Teeing Off to the Green
Using Golf as a Business Tool

Judy Anderson

Foreword by John Glozek, Jr.
of Long Island Golfer Magazine

Arrowhead Classics Publishers
P.O. Box 4189 □ Sevierville, Tennessee 37864

Contents

Preface

I've always been curious about the concept of business golf. More than twenty years ago, I marveled that my boss would choose to play golf every Saturday with the man who was his main adversary the rest of the week. I sensed that something was going on out there other than golf. Throughout my years of experience in education, sales, and corporate training, I continued to observe that golf and business were often intertwined.

As an independent consultant, I've worked to empower people through a variety of "success skills," conducting workshops and seminars on interpersonal communication skills. But the link between golf and business kept coming up. Finally, I discussed it with a sports psychologist who suggested I do some preliminary research to see if the link really existed. The result is this book.

The hundreds of business golfers I interviewed confirmed what I suspected. The business golf link is real. A lot of business is done on the golf course. But as one executive put it, "Business golf is the best kept secret in business!"

Until now, the fortunate people were introduced to the secret by a mentor. The rest learned by trial-and-error (and lost business along the way) or didn't take it seriously (and missed out on business). Even though I sensed the link was real, I didn't take it seriously when I was first starting my career - the opportunities for women to do so were rather limited them. Although I learned the game and became a recreational golfer, I didn't use it as a business tool then.

Now the secret is out. Veteran business golfers have shared their success strategies with me. I listened. I learned that business golf is also a "success skill" - it can help lead to success in business, but only if you have the skills. So I combined what the experts had to say with my experience and background in business, training, and counseling psychology, and I wrote this book. I hope you find the many opportunities that business golf has to offer. Above all, I hope you have fun with the game in the process.

Judy Anderson
New York, 1997

For information about Judy Anderson's professional speaking and consulting services or to share your experiences, stories, or comments about business golf, write or call:

Anderson Consulting & Training
107 Melville Road, Suite 2
Farmingdale, NY 11735
(516) 249-4814

Acknowledgments

Thanks to all the business golfers and teaching pros who took the time to share their stories and insights about business golf with me. I could not cite all of you in the text, but without you this book would not have been possible.

I would like to acknowledge the experts, researchers, and authors cited in the text and in the Resource Section, especially Tony Alessandra, and also the Hyatt Corporation.

I also want to thank my entire support system. Whether you served as mentor, colleague, editor, or friend, I really appreciate your help, support, and encouragement.

Foreword

Ever since I was a boy I had absolutely no interest in golf. I had better things to do, like playing football, baseball, hockey and, probably scariest of all to my parents, becoming a musician. My dad had played (and loved) golf for almost his entire life and tried many times to get me to take up the game. Placing a small driver in my crib didn't even help.

Decades went by and my life as a musician was pretty much set; right until I decided to get a job in corporate America. I worked for a large defense contractor that employed almost 40,000 people worldwide. For some strange reason I decided that if I had to work that hard from nine to five, I was going to run the place some day. A big "if" for someone who had only one wool suit and a tie to match.

It wasn't long before my boss came to me and said, "We need a fourth for Thursday. Do you play golf?" With only the slightest, possibly undetectable hesitation, I said, "Sure, I'll play." I immediately called my dad and told him I needed to borrow *his* clubs and that I had told my boss I play golf. I believe his reaction was more than surprised. In my opinion, I think I played just as poorly that day as the other three!

It wasn't long before I was invited to play again and said to myself, "Either I can work my butt off and be paid or I can play golf with my boss and be paid." I quickly caught on to the concept of going to play golf and still receiving a paycheck each week. Is this country great or what?

Really though, if it wasn't for my getting a job in corporate America and realizing how important golf is to corporate business, I probably would not be playing today. Now my involvement and love for the game goes well beyond just playing. After buying my first set of clubs at age 28 and spending days and nights out on the range, I started a regional golf magazine, *Long Island Golfer Magazine*, in one of the largest and busiest golf section in the entire country. It has given me the opportunity to see just what is out there in the corporate golf world.

One of my favorite stories is from an interview with the CEO and President of a major airline. Ironically, the interview and meeting took place at a golf course. The question I asked was simple, "How much business do you conduct on the golf course?" The answer was just as simple, "I have bought every plane I own on the golf course."

I was amazed by the answer and now include the question in many interviews. After hundreds of interviews, I've concluded this -- golf is a big business and golf is big for business. You should give it a try today.

In this book, Judy Anderson has done a wonderful job compiling everything you need to help you come out a winner... whether it's your golf game or business golf game, and whether you are a golfer or not.

I hope to see you out on the course.

John J. Glozek, Jr.
Publisher, *Long Island Golfer Magazine*

Introduction
The Business Golf Link

Many years ago, long before personal computers, fax machines, e-mail, rightsizing, and career management, *How to Succeed in Business Without Really Trying* first opened on Broadway. Even back then, I doubt that very many people succeeded without really trying or without having some business skills.

Since the early sixties when that show originally ran, the nature of business has changed dramatically. So has what it takes to succeed. Whatever your career path, you need a wide variety of technical, administrative, and human relations skills, many of which weren't even around a few short decades ago.

One business tool that was used back then, but primarily by upper management, is now available to everyone. Although this tool can give you a very definite competitive edge, it is not taught in business schools and is often not treated as the valuable tool that it is. In case the title of this book didn't tip you off, I'm talking about business golf.

The business golf link isn't a big surprise to most of us. We've all seen cartoons of the executive in an office putting a golf ball into a water glass. And Hollywood often depicts deals being made on the golf course. Still, many people don't take business golf seriously.

If you look beyond the stereotypes, you'll discover that golf really is a powerful business tool. In a recent study, "Golf and the Business Executive: An Attitudinal Study by Hyatt Hotels and Resorts," more than a third of senior-level executives said they had made some of their biggest deals on the golf course. These executives were also almost unanimous in agreeing that playing golf with a client is a good way to build a business relationship.

These very real business benefits are not limited to senior-level executives. The business golf link started to grow beyond the traditional bastion of the old-boy network beginning in the early sixties. Thanks in part to Arnold Palmer, Jack Nicklaus, Mark McCormack, and *Shell's Wonderful World of Golf*, the game now has mass appeal. Many recreational golfers, regardless of occupation or income level, have recognized the benefits of combining golf with business. And many non-golfers, male and female, have recognized the business opportunities that exist on the golf course.

The National Golf Foundation indicates that about 40 percent of new golfers are women. Judging from the number of businesswomen's golf associations that have formed, many of these women are taking the game up for business purposes. Another study by Korn-Ferry International, an executive search firm, surveyed over 400 female executives with average earnings over $180,000. These women reported that golf helped them move into the executive network and gave them better rapport with both clients and bosses.

Savvy executives have always known the secret to success in business. They understand this: Your success in business depends as much on your ability to build relationships as it does on your technical skills. That concept, incidentally, was one of the points made in *How to Succeed in Business Without Really Trying*!

Business golf can expand your network, establish your image as a team member, and help you build relationships and trust bonds in a way that few other activities can. Still, many executives underestimate the value of golf as a business tool. Some don't use it at all. Others damage business relationships and even lose business because they lack business golf skills. They don't understand that just as networking involves more than talking business at a cocktail party, business golf is much more than just combining business talk with driving, chipping, and putting.

In the past, business golf skills were developed in several ways. Some people were naturals. Others grew up in the country club environment where playing golf with business associates is practically a way of life. Still others learned the skills through the risky process of trial-and-error that sometimes damaged their business image.

This book was written to help you benefit from the experience of veteran business golfers and to help you avoid costly mistakes. Its purpose is to increase your awareness of the power of golf as a business tool and to help you become an effective business golfer.

It is designed to give you an overview of the game itself as well as an understanding of the various aspects of business golf. Stories, statistics, and quotes have been included to give you a flavor of the game and some insight into how golfers feel about it. A Resource Section is also included so you can follow up on topics that are of special interest to you.

If you've never played, it is important to keep in mind that business golf combines the complex skill of golf with the equally complex interpersonal skills of business communication and relationship building. Don't try to remember all the details or master all these skills at once! Take a tip from the legendary Bobby Jones who said it took him years to realize that golf is played one stroke at a time. Go about learning business golf one step at a time. First, read through the entire book to get a feel for the nature of business golf. Then focus on learning the fundamentals of the game itself. Once you've learned the basics of recreational golf, you can then refer back to the specific chapters that cover the various aspects of business golf.

How involved you become in business golf is up to you. But if you use the strategies presented, you will become a proficient business golfer even if you never become a great player. The strategies have worked for others and they can work for you. More important, you will develop a genuine appreciation and respect for the game - as a sport and as a business strategy.

Whether you're a novice or have been playing for years, I hope the information in this book will encourage you to find ways in which you can make the incredible tool of business golf work for you.

A Marriage Made In Heaven
Why Business Fell in Love With Golf

Winston Churchill thought golf was like "chasing a quinine pill around a cow pasture." It has also been described as a lot of walking broken up by disappointment and bad arithmetic. So why has business become so enchanted with this game that it has actually become a way of doing business?

I have my own theory. I believe that we've been subtly programmed over a thirty-year period to associate fun, wealth, success, and business with golf. And this was done at a time when our subconscious minds were very susceptible - just before we went to sleep - by Johnny Carson using a golf swing to take us into that first commercial break every night!

None of the executives or Professional Golf Association (PGA) pros I interviewed mentioned Johnny Carson as the reason for the business golf link. But they did have a lot of other good reasons why business and golf are a perfect match.

The Time Frame and Pace of the Game

Almost everyone I spoke with mentioned that the four-to-five hour time frame and leisurely pace of a round was great for getting to know someone and moving toward business.

Mike Marchev, who developed golf outings for Merrill Lynch for several years and now has his own consulting business, summed it up perfectly: " 'Can I meet with you?' buys about twenty minutes of time with phones ringing and secretaries interrupting. 'Let's play golf,' buys you five hours of real quality time. Time that allows you to develop rapport, continue to build a relationship, and move toward, and perhaps even do, business - all at a very leisurely pace."

The time frame also provides another advantage: the opportunity to observe someone over an extended period of time and in many different situations. Veteran business golfers know you can learn more about someone in one round of golf than you can in several months in an office setting. Golf reveals character and is a great opportunity to learn about people and how they react to the good and the bad breaks of the game.

The pace of golf is also perfect for doing business. A very small amount of the time spent on the golf course is actually devoted to hitting the ball. The time spent in the golf cart or walking to the next shot is perfect for getting to know someone. This laid-back pace is what appeals to many executives who spend the majority of their time in a very fast-paced, hustle-and- bustle environment.

As Ken Blanchard states in *Playing the Great Game of Golf - Making Every Minute Count*, the golf course is one of the few places that still allows us this "in-between" time. The breathers from business we used to enjoy have been pretty much eliminated by the fax machine, e-mail, and cellular phones. The golf course allows executives to get away from all of that, relax, unwind, have fun, and still have the opportunity to do some business. Add to this the fact that you can play with just about anyone and it becomes even more apparent why golf is so popular with the business community.

The Democratic Nature of the Game

To really enjoy most games, you have to play with someone whose skill level is similar to yours. So even if tennis and racquetball are favorites of some business executives, their usefulness as a business tool is really limited. Because of the nature of golf and the handicap system, you can play an enjoyable, even challenging round with anyone, regardless of skill level.

And because various side games are so popular in golf, even someone brand new to the game can come out a winner.

Because of the relaxed pace of golf and the nature of the physical requirements, there is no age limit to the game. Members of the board of directors, who are often retired senior-level executives, and up-and-coming junior-level executives can play a round together that everyone enjoys and finds challenging.

The Setting

Another reason many people play well into their golden years is also one executives give for combining business with golf. That is the setting - the natural appeal of the golf course.

It was golf pro Walter Hagen who first reminded us that "life is much too short. Make sure to take time and smell the flowers along the way." The golf course is the perfect place to do this. The beauty of the great outdoors helps put most people into a relaxed state of mind. This is often much more conducive to doing business than is an office.

The golf course also provides an informal atmosphere, with a much greater sense of privacy than exists in an office setting. Several executives told me that they have found certain business matters easier to discuss or certain individuals easier to talk to because of the unpretentious scene. It is almost as though the casual, off-the-record nature of the setting makes the business talk less critical and so there is less chance that egos get involved. There is something about golf that promotes camaraderie, even if you sit on opposite sides of the table at business. And if egos do get involved, it is more often because of the game itself than the business!

The Challenging and Competitive Nature of Golf

Throughout its history, golf has been associated with the wealthy and with those in business. Thanks in large part to Arnold Palmer and televised tournaments, golf is no longer just a game for the well-to-do. But it is still a game that is very attractive to people in business. This may be because the challenges of golf in many ways parallel the challenges of business.

In golf as in no other sport, you compete against yourself, others, and the environment in much the same way you do in business. The challenge and focus is on achieving your own personal best, not on beating others. But in the process, you do win out over your competition. This is the concept behind the handicap system in golf; this is the concept behind total quality management in business. The focus on personal best is at least partially the result of golf being a closed rather than an open skill sport.

Tennis, for example, is basically an open skill sport where one person reacts to the other person's shots. What I do is dependent on what you do. Golf, however, is a closed skill. My action is not dependent on your action. The focus is on action rather than reaction to what someone else did. The action is influenced, however, by the environment and how it impacts the actions of others. For example, your club choice will depend on the wind (environment) and how the wind affected the shots of the other players. This is all very similar to what happens in business, where your actions may depend on the economy, your competitors' actions, and the outcome of those actions in terms of the economy. This type of environmental influence is found in very few sports other than golf.

sports are played on a standardized playing area. Not so with
.ch golf course is different. Even the same course is always
.it because of varying weather conditions and different hole
plac..nent. Reading the ever-changing environment, analyzing the
feedback you receive, and adapting to an environment that's not always
fair are the challenges of the game - the game of golf and the game of
business! Golf allows you to use a combination of left brain-right brain
skills that are also used in business to meet this challenge. And it provides
a great opportunity to see how others react to the demands of the
challenge.

Golf as a Revealer of Character

As I mentioned earlier, spending four to five hours on the golf course
with someone is a great way to really get to know them and to observe
them in many different situations. When you understand how closely the
game simulates business, you can gather a wealth of information about a
person during one round of golf. This link between golf behavior and
business behavior was the focus of the Hyatt Study, "Golf and the
Business Executive: An Attitudinal Study by Hyatt Hotels and Resorts."
The study found that most of the executives surveyed did rate themselves
similarly as both golfers and business people on business-related
characteristics.

This is the aspect of golf that makes it such a valuable business tool.
And this is the aspect of golf that can turn it into a lethal weapon if *you*
reveal character traits that are less than desirable because you haven't
mastered the principles of business golf.

As you can see, there are many logical reasons why golf and business
are a perfect match. But if you know human nature, you know that
decisions are not made logically; they are made emotionally. We then use
the logical reasons to provide a rationale for our emotionally based
decision. It is the same with golf. There are many logical reasons for the
business golf link. But when you come right down to it, golf's popularity
is based on emotions. People just love the game, because even with all its
frustrations, it is still an esteem builder.

Golf as an Esteem Builder

Ask people what they think of when they think of golf and you'll
probably get the same kinds of answers I did. Most people think it is pretty
classy. And there is something about golf attitudes and life-style that
reflects prestige, class, and power. These positive associations are
longstanding and probably began with golf's close ties to the old-boy
network.

For whatever reason, golf is perceived by many as the in thing, the classy thing to do.

So when you invite someone to a round of business golf, you, in essence, are holding them in a position of esteem. Think about it. How would *you* feel about someone who invited you to bowl a few frames versus someone who invited you to a round of golf at a prestigious private club?

People love golf because it makes them feel special. And when you can make money doing something you love, you've fulfilled at least part of the American dream!

Other Business Sports

But is golf the only sport associated with business? Certainly not. There are several other sports that are also used as business tools, but none really has the broad appeal of golf.

Tennis

Next to golf, tennis is the sport that was most used as a business tool by the executives I interviewed. The obvious limitation is the need to have someone close to your skill level to really enjoy the game. Age is another limiting factor with tennis. Further, the pace of the game is really not conducive to doing business, except maybe at lunch afterward.

Tennis as a spectator sport is a very popular form of client entertainment, especially in parts of the country where major tournaments are held. Tennis does have the same aura of class and prestige as golf, so it is a good business match in that respect. However, because of its limitations, the business use of tennis is not broad.

Sand Volleyball

Several meeting planners told me that many of their clients now request sand volleyball as a group activity at off-site conferences and outings. This can be a great team-building activity and rapport builder. Unfortunately, not everyone can participate because of many of the same limitations that are found in tennis. And how often can you use sand volleyball for client entertainment?

Bowling

Bowling has long been used as an employee activity. It is an effective means of informal team building and can help employees develop better working relationships. Bowling probably has the most in common with golf. It is a closed skill and there is really no age limit to enjoying the game. However, the image bowling projects is a major drawback to its use as a business tool. As mentioned, bowling is just not the esteem builder that golf is.

Boating, Yachting, and Charter Fishing

Sailing, yachting, and charter fishing are great forms of client entertainment. You have the advantages of the extended time frame, a beautiful setting, and certainly, an esteem builder. Sailing can also be adapted into a formalized team-building activity. For example, South Seas Plantation Resort in Captiva, Florida has an Off Shore Sailing School that provides a six-day team-building program for corporate groups. The major drawback of using these water sports for business purposes is their limited accessibility - both geographically and financially.

Croquet

You may be as surprised at this one as I was, but croquet is growing in popularity as a business sport. According to meeting planners I spoke with, more and more corporate clients are requesting croquet at their conferences. The number of resorts that offers this sport is rapidly growing. The leader seems to be Meadowood Resort in California's Napa Valley. They even offer guests the services of a resident croquet pro! Croquet does have many of the advantages of golf, so it may become the next big business sport. But outside of the resort setting, it seems its use in client entertainment could be somewhat limited.

Perhaps you can think of other sports that are also used for business purposes. Many are. Use as many as you can. They can all be valuable business tools. But none are as versatile and offer as many advantages as golf. That is probably why the interest in golf as a business tool keeps growing.

Possible Reasons for the Increasing Interest in Business Golf

As I asked various business golfers about the reasons for the business golf link, I noticed a pattern developing. Over and over, they would mention the reasons we've already looked at. A few people, however, came up with their own rather unique theories or reasons why the interest in golf has grown so incredibly in recent years.

Several executives speculated that business golf is more helpful if you are in a service industry than in a product-oriented industry. Since you don't have a product to demonstrate and are basically selling yourself and your credibility, the relationship becomes even more important. Where better to develop the relationship than on the golf course!

Both meeting planners and executives mentioned that the client or employee who is being entertained seems to place a greater value on business golf during hard times. The rationale goes something like this: Business golf is expensive, but it hasn't been cut from the budget. It is getting executives out of the office at a time when they may be most needed there because of rightsizing. So *it* must be important and *they* must be important. This greater perceived value also creates a greater likelihood of reciprocity: the employee works harder, the client is more apt to do business with you. This may lead corporate America to also perceive that the value of golf as a business tool is greater during hard times.

The senior vice president of one of the major commercial banks in the New York Metropolitan area also believes the economy is responsible for the increased interest in business golf, but for a different reason. Many of his clients are new entrepreneurs who wear many hats, face many new challenges, and often have driving personalities. The bank vice president believes the best way to do business with entrepreneurs is to get them away from their desks and on to a golf course. In his experience, they welcome the break and value the opportunity more than they would have when they were a cog in the corporate machine. This ties in very closely with the perceived value theory!

A few people offered ideas about the increased interest in business golf outings. The increased interest in golf as an employee development tool may be closely related to the "work as a game" movement. This use of golf has increased greatly in the last few years and coincides with the increased understanding of the parallels between golf and business.

Or outings may be more popular because recent rightsizing has made it impossible for many people to justify taking the time for a round of golf unless it is part of corporate group outing.

Finally, the increased interest may be a variation of the "stop to smell the roses" idea. Many people have reassessed their priorities for the nineties and may have a desire to get more fun out of business. This is on target with the trend Faith Popcorn talks about in *The Popcorn Report*. As jobs become more and more demanding, people question their priorities. The trend is to find more enjoyment in work, reduce stress as much as possible, and adapt and combine activities to provide the most satisfaction possible. Business golf fits the bill on all counts.

Summary

Whatever the reasons for the ever-increasing interest in golf, the fact remains that golf and business have been closely linked for many years.

Because of the time frame and relaxed pace of the game, the setting, the challenges it offers, and the opportunity it provides to really get to know someone, golf can be a valuable business tool. Although other sports can also be used for business purposes, none have the versatility or popularity of golf. It seems highly unlikely that golf and business will ever be separated. The business golf link is truly a match made in heaven.

Surveying the Course
Kinds of Business That Are Done
on the Golf Course

Golf may be just an expensive way to play marbles, as a bumper sticker I saw recently suggested. But it is also a cost-effective way to meet a variety of business objectives. This chapter discusses the many ways in which golf can be used in business. These include:

- **Networking**
- **Recruiting**
- **Establishing rapport and building relationships**
- **Resolving current or potential problems**
- **Employee development**
- **Goodwill, public relations, and advertising**

Networking

Playing with strangers or acquaintances you don't know very well may not seem like business golf, but you never know whom you might meet on the golf course. Because of golf's prestigious image and its association with the old-boy network, you can often get to know people you couldn't meet in any other way. This is especially true if you are playing at a private club.

Before you use golf for networking, it is important to really understand how networking works. Too often people expect magic from it - immediate solutions to their problems by way of a done deal. Instead, networking provides you with contacts, who have contacts, who have contacts, etcetera. In most cases, it is the contact three or four levels removed that will end up being the person you want to do business with and it will take time to meet that person and to develop the relationship.

If you have this realistic expectation, you'll find that the golf course is an excellent place to network. There is still always the possibility that the person you are playing with *is* the one who can help you, which is just icing on the cake!

Golf has been successfully used to network for jobs, prospects or clients, and mentors. One young executive I spoke with had interviewed with a company for a position but was not very hopeful that he would get it. Through strategic networking (knowing someone who knew someone who could set up a golf date), he ended up in a foursome that included the president and chief executive officer of the company he had interviewed with. The CEO was impressed with the young man's character and intelligence (and his scratch golf!) and told him to come in the next day. He got the job and is now building a great career with the company.

An assistant pro at a private club who couldn't get a job in his college major (accounting) because of the recession, received five offers from club members for accounting positions within his first year as a pro!

You can also use your golf network to find a mentor. Once you've identified the individual you believe could be your mentor, place that person in a mentor-type role by asking for advice or suggestions on course management, club selection, or anything else golf-related. Do it in a sincere manner and as an equal. The relationship that develops over time can be very helpful, with your mentor networking for you and helping you cut through a lot of the red tape usually involved in meeting senior-level people.

Probably the most common objective for networking on the golf course is to find prospects and clients for your business. The majority of executives I spoke with mentioned using golf in this way. So if you are not good at networking, now is the time to brush up on those skills.

Tips for Networking on the Golf Course

I can just hear some of you saying that it is the old story of "It's not what you know, it's who you know." It is really an update of that story: "It's who knows what you know." It is really pretty basic human nature. People usually want to help others if they like the other person, understand what the other person wants, believe the other person would help them in return, and know they aren't being manipulated by the other person. So follow these simple points to get the most from networking on the golf course.

1. Take a hint from Dale Carnegie. Go out with the goal of winning friends and influencing people, not with the hope of reeling in a big one. This will help keep it all in perspective.

2. Don't let the networking interfere with anyone's golf game.
3. Know what you want and what you have to offer. Have a clear, concise, interesting statement ready in case anyone asks you.
4. If no one does, ask them an appropriate question to start the conversation. Do this without interfering with their golf game.
5. Talk in terms of what you can do for someone else, not in terms of what someone else can do for you.
6. Always carry your business card and ask for the other person's card.
7. Don't expect immediate results.

Although jobs, clients, and mentors are the main business golf reasons for networking, the sky's the limit for on-course networking. For example, local golf contacts can be helpful in providing contacts who are members of private clubs in other cities. That really makes it convenient to play at great courses when you are traveling. And there is always the possibility that these new relationships could also lead to business.

Of course, you'll also use networking on the golf course the way you would use any networking opportunity: to find a good electrician, accountant, plumber, or contractor. Whether your business is enhanced by additional revenue or by getting a better deal on a product or service you need, it is still business golf because someone's business benefits as a result of the networking.

Recruiting

Another business function that often takes place on the golf course is recruiting. Imagine you are applying for a position with a company, have had the initial interview, and are called back for a second or third interview. How would you feel about a company that suggested a round of golf at a beautiful course as part of the interview process? You would probably be pretty impressed and come away with the idea that it is a good company to work for. Even if you didn't get the job, you would still probably have a very positive image of that company.

These are just some of the reasons many companies use golf as part of the recruiting and interviewing process. It projects the prestigious kind of image a corporation wants to have. In addition, a round of golf gives the corporate executives four to five hours to observe you. This gives them a lot more information about you than they could ever get during an interview in an office setting or even over lunch.

If the job involves business golf with clients, using golf as an applicant screening tool also gives the prospective employer information on how you'd handle that situation.

With all these advantages, it is obvious why more and more companies are using golf in this way.

Establishing Rapport and Building Relationships

Many executives may tell you they don't believe in doing business on the golf course. But when they think about it, they acknowledge that a large part of their client base was developed during a round of golf. Golf is such a great way to develop a relationship and build rapport that this is probably the primary way many people use it. Prospect and client entertainment on the golf course is no doubt one of the most popular forms of business entertainment.

When playing with a prospect, the goal is usually to develop the relationship so you can do business. With a client, the objective could be making sure things are going well, expressing your appreciation for business you've already received, or developing more business. A more sophisticated way of saying thank you is to help your clients enhance *their* business by using the round to help them build *their* network and to enlarge their client base. You can accomplish this by choosing the other members of the foursome very carefully to include people your client can do business with. The final result will often be that you will also come away with additional business. At the very least, you will probably also end up with a client who is willing to network on your behalf.

Resolving Current or Potential Problems

Golf is also great for repairing difficult relationships or avoiding problems down the line.

In today's competitive economy, it is not unusual to lose a client. Playing with that former client is an excellent way to work on a strained relationship and find out what you can do to regain the business. Even if you don't end up with the business, you'll still come away with a better idea of how your product or service stacks up against your competition. You'll also have important feedback that can help in modifying your strategy, if necessary.

A round of golf can also help resolve difficult situations. When problems exist in business relationships or when business circumstances place you on the opposing team, golf can be a way for people to see each other as something other than adversaries. A club pro tells of two members of his club who had a business relationship that had soured to the point that they were no longer speaking. A third club member who knew both approached one of the executives and suggested that he give the offending party another chance and at least get back on speaking terms by playing in a foursome together. The time spent during that round was enough to thaw the relationship without anyone losing face. The business relationship was salvaged.

Now you may say the same thing could have happened by getting the two parties together in an office or over lunch. Maybe it could, but it's more likely to happen on the golf course because of all those special advantages golf offers. First of all, the agenda was golf and each person had a challenging game and two other people to focus on, so the possibility of a direct confrontation was reduced and the situation was less threatening. The time frame allowed the process to happen at its own pace. And the relaxed atmosphere allowed everyone to see each other as real people rather than simply as business associates. It is a lot harder for all this to happen in an hour over lunch.

Before Stewart Meyer became President and CEO of the Saint Louis Cardinals baseball team, he held a human resources position with Anheuser-Busch and was heavily involved with labor relations and union negotiations. He beautifully summed up how golf can impact a potentially difficult relationship: "Golf helped in keeping a good relationship, so even if you disagreed, you weren't perceived as a bad person. They liked you, respected you, and got to know you, even if you were on opposite sides of an issue."

This rationale is also part of the reason business golf has assumed such a major role in employee development in recent years.

Employee Development

Golf has long been associated with business in terms of employee incentives and rewards and as an employee benefit. Sales incentive awards have very often been trips to exotic destinations that typically include a stay at a beautiful golf resort. Some companies even recognize the value of golf as a regular employee activity. IBM, for example, is just one company that until recently had its own golf course. Other companies, such as McGraw-Hill Inc., have executive golf leagues for employees in much the same way that some companies sponsor employee softball teams or bowling leagues.

As management theories began to focus on the importance of teamwork and on business as a game, parallels were drawn between business and various sports. Golf parallels business in many ways that no other sport can and is adaptable for employee development purposes as few other sports are. The reasons why are much the same as those mentioned in Chapter 1.

Anyone can play regardless of age or skill level. Even if some of the employees don't play at all, events such as putting contests and monkey golf can be adapted in various ways to meet the objectives of the group and allow everyone to participate. And, unlike some other currently popular methods of team building, such as mountain climbing and white water rafting, there is very little physical danger involved. Increased insurance claims and workers' compensation cases are often the high price businesses pay for those more physically challenging team-building activities.

The competitive nature of golf more closely resembles the nature of business than most other sports do. Unlike most sports that are played on a standard playing area, each golf course is different, just as each business situation is different. The goal is to understand and master the situation, which changes from hole to hole. As one executive told me, "In golf and in business, it's just you who takes final responsibility."

One round of golf can, and very often does, provide a wide range of experiences. Any golfer will tell you that it is typical to have such a bad hole that you want to give up the game, and then a few holes later, play so well you are ready to join the PGA tour. This rollercoaster ride from ridiculous to sublime parallels many business situations. How employees deal with it on the golf course often reflects how they deal with it in the business setting.

Golf is not as reactive as other sports. The golfer initiates the action of hitting a ball that's not in motion. In other sports, the challenge is very often to react to the ball that is coming your way. This reaction allows for a release of tension. In contrast, the careful setup that is required to initiate the golf swing does not release tension, but can often create it. Golf's initiation of action based on a reaction (to the course and the elements) parallels the complex responses that are often required in business.

Every shot counts. In some other sports, you can get away with playing poorly because bad shots can get buried in the final score. Although in golf you can play a bad hole and still come out with a good round, the scorecard is permanent feedback on every shot hit during the round. This aspect of golf is in line with the current focus in business on excellence and total quality management.

Golf can be adapted to meet employee development needs. In structured team building, the group can spend some time in a classroom setting discussing what they hope to learn from the round. The round is then structured to highlight these specific business skills. For example, monkey golf can focus on the group dynamics of decision making. A debriefing after the round helps the group to see the parallels between golf behavior and business behavior and allows them to develop strategies for using this new information in the business setting.

No other sport or activity combines all these advantages and allows for employee development the way golf does. Little wonder so many companies are using it as a team-building tool.

Goodwill, Public Relations, and Advertising

The most visible way many companies use business golf is in public relations, advertising, and building goodwill. The possibilities for this use of business golf are virtually limitless and can be adapted to your specific business needs, whether you are an entrepreneur or the CEO of a Fortune 500 company. Both on the local and national level, this kind of business golf centers around golf outings or golf events.

You can use local golf outings to build goodwill, promote, and advertise your business by donating prizes, sponsoring ads in a program, or purchasing a tee, which gives you the privilege of having your company's name on display at that tee during the outing. Larger companies can donate a big prize (usually a car or a large sum of money) for a hole-in-one scored on a particular hole. (The company usually buys hole-in-one insurance to cover the high cost of the prize in case someone does make a hole-in-one!).

If you watch professional golf on TV, you are very familiar with corporate sponsorship of tour events. Another popular way to keep your corporate name in front of the public is by having a golf pro endorse your product and wear something with your company's name and logo on it during the event. Hospitality tents at larger events are another great way to build goodwill and are also a very effective form of client entertainment.

Of course, whenever business golf is conducted effectively, goodwill will be a natural result. People will automatically hold you in higher esteem because of the fun they had playing golf with you!

Summary

Although many people think of business golf in terms of prospect and client entertainment, a variety of other business functions have been successfully combined with golf. Golf is an effective business tool that has many applications, limited only by your own imagination. Based on the application you are using, you'll want to choose the most effective format. In the next chapter, we'll look at several variations beyond the traditional foursome.

How To Drive Home The Business
The Many Ways Golf Is Used in Business

One of the challenges of golf is deciding which of the fourteen clubs you'll use for a particular shot. With most games, you only have one piece of equipment (a racquet, bat, hockey stick, etcetera) that you use throughout the entire game. In golf, you determine your objective and decide which club will serve you best in reaching that objective.

In much the same way, "business golf" includes various formats and is really an entire set of tools. Once you've defined your objective (possibly one of the business functions discussed in Chapter 2), the next step is to decide the type of business golf that will serve you best in reaching that objective.

The basic objective in club selection is picking the club that will get the ball to the target. But to reach your decision, you'll consider the distance, the lie of the ball (how the ball is positioned on the ground), wind conditions, your expertise and preferences, and your past experience. And some of these variables will changes from time to time, from hole to hole, and from course to course. To really play well, you need to thoughtfully go through this decision process each time you select a club.

Likewise, in business golf, you'll want to define your objective as carefully as possible to make sure you maximize the golf experience. Consider the various formats of business golf that might help you reach your objective. Then weigh your options in terms of such variables as your budget, time constraints, approximate dollar value of the outcome you expect, the skill and interest level of the client or employee, and the message the business golf experience will communicate.

For example, if your objective is networking or prospecting, you could either play a round at a public course or you could attend a local chamber of commerce outing. You would decide which type of business golf could help you more by weighing several factors, such as a cost of about $20 compared to $150; about five hours of your time versus a whole day spent away from the office; and the opportunity to meet three people compared to the opportunity to meet 143 business and community leaders. You probably can think of other variables that would help with your decision. The considerations will change based on your objective, the industry you are in, and the client or employee you may be entertaining. What doesn't change is the need to make a *business decision* about how to use this business tool. If you view it as recreational golf rather than as business golf, you could fall into the trap of making a decision on an emotional basis, according to what you'd enjoy most - and that isn't always best for business!

Before you can go through this process, you'll want to be familiar with the various formats of business golf. Although inviting a client to play a round of golf is the traditional format, outings and celebrity golf are becoming more and more popular.

Playing a Round

Playing a round is probably the most common method of using business golf because it is so accessible. You can invite a client or employee to play a round of golf just about anytime, anywhere, and with very little advance notice. It is usually less structured than an outing or celebrity golf, and since fewer people are involved, it is a great opportunity to really get to know someone.

Because it is usually the least expensive form of business golf, it is perceived by the client as less of an event than an outing or celebrity golf. This may mean that the client is more relaxed and less guarded about your motives, which can make it a lot easier to build rapport and develop a relationship.

When you invite someone to play business golf, you want to create the most positive experience possible. This usually requires some advance planning. You'll want to consider the person's skill level and interest in golf, decide on the course you want to play, determine who else should be included in the foursome, and decide on an appropriate 19th hole activity. Chapter 9 discusses all this in detail and also gives you some helpful hints for when you are the guest. But before you decide to extend the invitation, you'll want to be aware of all your options. Maybe there is an outing coming up soon that would more effectively help you reach your objective.

Golf Outings

Golf outings are planned events that involve a group of golfers, often include activities other than golf, and may include national or international travel. Generally, golf outings are either corporate-sponsored or set up as fund-raisers by civic or charitable organizations.

Corporate-Sponsored Outings

Leagues. Employee golf leagues are offered by some companies in much the same way employee bowling leagues are. However, higher level executives are more likely to participate in golf than bowling. The leagues offer a great opportunity to network with high-level executives you normally wouldn't have access to, learn about the company, and possibly find a mentor. Companies view golf leagues as an informal team-building activity that can improve morale, strengthen working relationships, and get employees involved with golf as a business tool.

If your company is interested in starting a golf league, local golf pros can help with the details.

However, although golf leagues serve a purpose in employee development and are growing in popularity, they do have some drawbacks. The number of employees who can participate is limited and mostly includes those who are really into golf and those in professional positions or at the mid-management to senior level. Because the league meets after business hours, some employees may find the time or location inconvenient or may be unwilling to make the time commitment necessary. To gain the benefits of a league without the disadvantages, some companies choose to sponsor tournaments instead.

Local Tournaments. Tournaments are usually set up as half-day or one-day events and offer much more flexibility than leagues do. Best of all, tournaments can include prospects and clients as well as employees. They can also be structured according to the specific objectives you want to achieve.

Employee tournaments can be used as a sales or performance incentive or reward, and as an informal team-building effort. Employees often perceive this as a fun day away from the office and a business perk akin to the company picnic or Christmas party. Employees who have never played golf can be included and can have a positive experience, because side games can be set up and the rules can be adapted so everyone can play. Prizes, trophies, and lunch or dinner are usually included as part of the event.

If the company's objective is employee development and team building, the tournament can be structured to provide a much different type of experience, as mentioned in Chapter 3. In this case, the participants are usually very carefully selected and assigned to foursomes based on their membership or potential membership on the work or management team. Very often some classroom instruction on roles and team interaction precede the round. A special format of play is often adopted to facilitate the learning and a classroom debriefing follows the round. This use of an employee tournament usually makes the learning points by focusing on group dynamics as well as on the parallels between the competitive nature of both golf and business.

There are many possibilities for employee tournaments that fall somewhere between these two examples. The tournament format allows for so much flexibility that the variations are almost endless. Although Chapter 10 provides specific information on setting up outings, your best bet is to rely on a professional planner or, if you're doing the planning in-house, your local golf pro. This will help ensure that the event is successful and all details are attended to. Since one of the basic objectives of business golf is providing a positive experience for the employee or client, you'll want to make sure there are no problems. This is especially true when you are entertaining prospects or clients. Having a professional help you organize the outing is the easiest way to do this.

Many companies use tournaments for client entertainment. Again, the format is flexible, but decisions regarding the invitation list and foursome groupings are even more critical than for employee outings. You'll want to very carefully consider the blend between employees, clients, and prospects to provide the most enjoyable experience and the best business opportunities for all concerned.

Because a tournament usually has a higher perceived value than a round of golf, you'll probably invite only your more valuable clients or prospects. Remember, one of the variables you'll always consider when deciding on the appropriate business golf format is the approximate dollar value of the expected outcome. In plain, modern lingo, you'll want to get the most bang for your buck!

Conferences/Meetings.   Some employees and clients are so valuable, you may decide something more than a local tournament is appropriate. That's when you'll look at what your company can offer in terms of conferences, meetings and excursions.

Companies have long used national and regional meetings in desirable locations as employee incentives and rewards. Today, the "desirable location" is often on a golf course, because more and more resorts now provide excellent meeting and convention facilities, and more and more people who attend meetings want to play.

Flexibility is the word when it comes to how business golf fits into your meeting agenda. Many companies include golf as a change of pace from technical meetings that often dominate the agenda. Other companies plan very structured team-building outings as part of the agenda, along with keynote speeches and breakout sessions on industry-related topics. Some companies strongly encourage everyone to participate in the golf event, while others view golf as one of several free time activities available.

Business golf at conferences and meetings really offers the same opportunities and options that exist with local tournaments and informal foursomes. The location, time frame, and cost are the major differences. The "off-site" location limits distractions that often exist when everyone is closer to home. The three to five day time frame allows for really in-depth relationship building at a relaxed pace. Also, the obvious cost involved labels it as a "special event" and communicates that the client or employee is important.

Although conferences and meetings are usually attended by employees, some companies also invite clients or vendors who may find the meetings helpful. More often, clients are invited on excursions rather than conferences or meetings.

Excursions. When employees or clients are invited to a golf resort and there is no formal agenda of business meetings, the outing is an excursion rather than a conference. The primary purpose of an excursion is entertainment, and it is often used as a "thank you" gesture to valuable clients and employees and as an incentive to continue the relationship in the future. Because of the focus on fun, the spouse or guest of the client or employee is usually also invited on an excursion. Depending on the agenda and number of meetings, this may or may not be the case at a conference.

The business golf on an excursion is almost always informal and less structured than the carefully planned activities on the agenda at a conference. Nevertheless, planning is essential to ensure that everyone has a good time and that there are no problems. Many travel agents now specialize in arranging golf excursions and can help with the planning. It is also helpful to check with the pro staff at the resort to make sure all goes well.

One way to cut down on your planning responsibilities is to participate in fund-raisers rather then sponsoring an excursion on your own. They also come in handy when corporate- sponsored events are just not practical because of the size of your organization or because of budgetary concerns.

Although fund-raisers are usually local and not as glamorous as excursions, they have broad business applications and have advantages that make them great business tools.

Fund-raisers

Many charitable, civic, and fraternal organizations have found that golf outings and tournaments are great fund-raisers. As fund-raisers have grown in popularity, the sponsoring organizations have had to become more competitive in order to attract participants. Therefore, the objective of most of these organizations is to provide a top-quality experience that will attract the most people at the highest price but will still be perceived as worth the cost. This often translates into an event that is held at an exclusive, private club that participants would love to play but don't usually have access to. This provides business golfers with a great opportunity to entertain clients or employees and also to network.

Buying a foursome. Most organizations that run golf fund-raisers will let you sign up as a single and will slot you into a foursome. This can be a great networking or prospecting opportunity.

Most often, however, the organization will ask you to put together a foursome. This can provide you (and your company) with a great way to host employees or clients without all the planning involved in running your own event.

Roger Gulley, an old pro at organizing fund-raisers, asks every golfer who signs up for his outings to be a "co-chairman" for the event. The only responsibility of the position is to put together a foursome. This makes Gulley's job easier, but business executives love it, too. They can buy or sponsor one or more foursomes themselves. Or, as a co-chairman, they can promote the event and encourage other business executives (employees, clients, suppliers) to participate at their own expense - it *is* for a worthy cause! This strategy allows you the flexibility to use the fund-raiser in much the same way you would use a corporate-sponsored event.

Before you sign up for a fund-raiser, be sure to get all the details. If possible, talk to someone who attended last year. If you are attending alone, you'll want to make sure it is a quality event that will attract the people you want to do business with. If you are putting together one or more foursomes, you'll want to be certain that you are providing the other golfers with a positive experience. Whether or not you pay for it, the people you invite to participate will associate *you* with the event. So you want to be sure it creates a positive impression.

Find out about the course, the format (shotgun start or assigned tee times, scramble or best ball, or any of the other variations described in Chapter 17), meal arrangements, other activities (such as putting contests or beat the pro), and prizes. Also get as much information as you can about who will be attending. The sponsoring organization will often share this with you even before you ask, because, as Gulley put it, the success of the outing depends on "marrying the right kinds of companies."

The information you gather will help you decide if you want to use this fund-raiser for business golf, and if so, whom you want to invite or encourage to attend. Inviting the right blend of people is just as important to the business golfer as getting the right companies to participate is to the outing sponsor. Chapter 10 will help you in dealing with all aspects of playing host at an outing.

If you believe a fund-raiser is worth attending, you may also want to use it to increase your visibility and enhance your business through advertising and publicity. When you sign up for a foursome, the outing sponsor will probably ask you if you are interested in any of these promotional opportunities.

Using fund-raisers to build goodwill. When you invite a business associate to a fund-raiser, goodwill is automatically created. Everyone feels good because they're contributing to a worthy cause. This can also create a special bond between people, as they feel they are partners in making the world a better place to live.

Your company can use this concept to even greater advantage by becoming a sponsor for the event. Depending on the outing, as discussed in Chapter 3, this is usually done by donating prizes, purchasing an ad in the program or journal, or purchasing a tee or hole (having your company's name displayed on a specific tee). This can be a great form of advertising and can sometimes lead to free publicity in the local media. It can increase a company's name recognition and also promotes the image that the company is socially aware. Make the decision to use this type of business golf carefully, based not only on cost-benefit, but also on the image of the sponsoring organization and the entire outing.

These promotional opportunities can also be a way to use business golf even if you don't play. Celebrity golf, which focuses more on golf as a spectator sport, is another popular way to do this.

Celebrity Golf

Most people enjoy meeting celebrities. For a golfer, one of the biggest thrills possible is watching a professional golfer play in person. The only thing that could top it is meeting the pro and maybe even playing a round with the pro! Business recognized this long ago and so celebrity golf has become a very effective form of business golf. It can be combined with corporate- sponsored events and fund-raisers to provide a business tool with even more impact.

Professional Events as Spectator Sports

Whether it is a PGA, Ladies Professional Golf Association (LPGA), or Senior PGA tour event, or a special tournament or local event that involves pros, celebrity golf events offer a wide range of business golf opportunities.

Very often people think of the golf event as the three rounds that are played on Friday, Saturday, and Sunday. For major events, this is what receives the majority of publicity and TV coverage because this is where the winner is determined. However, many professional golf events run the entire week.

Monday is often the qualifying event or arrival day. Tuesday the pros usually play a practice round and sometimes participate in a shoot-out or some other special event that is open to the public. Wednesday and Thursday are often devoted to a two-round pro-am, with teams of amateurs playing with the professionals.

Guest passes. Most golf events offer hospitality packages to corporate sponsors. This would include guest passes that the company could use for employee or client entertainment.

Guest passes allow fans to walk the course with the players or view play from behind the tees, greens, and along the fairways. Some events offer special passes for bleacher seating on certain holes. Also, certain areas are designated as handicapped viewing areas.

The cost and availability of tickets are based on the nature and national popularity of the event and the players who are participating. For example, tickets to the Northville Long Island Classic, a Senior PGA event, are not as expensive or difficult to get as tickets to the Doral-Ryder Open or The Masters.

Guest passes are usually available for specific days, for the weekend, or for the entire week. The type of pass is also considered when you decide whom to invite.

If your company does not purchase a hospitality package or block of passes, you can usually arrange to purchase individual passes for business entertainment prior to the event. Tickets are usually available through the sponsor or, for larger events, through a travel agent or company that specializes in golf outings.

In addition to guest passes, passes to a hospitality tent are often available. Larger companies can sponsor their own hospitality tent to further enhance the experience for their business guests.

Hospitality tents. Simply furnishing your clients with guest passes doesn't allow for a lot on one-on-one interaction. A hospitality tent provides the opportunity to get out of the sun, sit down, enjoy some refreshments, and possibly meet and network with company executives and other guests.

A pass to the hospitality tent is obviously considered a bigger privilege than a guest pass for admission to the event. It is helpful to have these different levels of options when you're deciding who will make the cut on your invitation list. If a client or employee is especially valuable, you may even consider a pro-am sponsorship.

If participation in a professional event as a spectator is a thrill, imagine what actually playing with the pros would be like! And imagine the impact it could have on a business relationship if you invite a client to play.

Pro-Am Competition

Most of the professional golf tournaments have a two-day event that allows amateurs to play with the pros. For many golfers, this is a dream come true. For business golfers, it is also an excellent opportunity to network with high-level executives. When it is used for client or employee entertainment, it sends the message loud and clear that the client or employee is important. And participants can get a lot of mileage out of the stories about the experience that they can use during future business golf opportunities.

The cost of participating in a pro-am competition varies according to the prestige associated with the professional event, but is always at least several thousand dollars. For this, the amateur golfer has the opportunity to meet and play with the pros. Typically, the pro-am package could also include golf clothing and equipment, souvenir items and photos taken with the pros.

Although pro-am competition has advantages for the business golfer, it is costly and opportunities to participate are limited by the number of professional events held and the number of amateur slots available. So corporations have found a more efficient way to provide the same kind of experience. Enter VIP golf.

VIP Golf

If it is good business to bring your clients or employees to a golf event where they can meet a pro, it is even better business to bring a pro to a business event where he or she can meet your clients or employees. This may be more cost-effective, and it definitely gives business more control in structuring the event.

When a company invites a golf pro to an outing, convention or meeting, it has great flexibility in terms of how many people can participate and what the level of participation will be. The pro can play a round with a limited number of business VIPs, conduct a skills clinic for a larger number of clients or employees, or attend a cocktail party and give an after-dinner speech so even non-golfers have a sense of participation. A corporation could also use VIP golf to reach large numbers of prospects and build goodwill and name recognition by sponsoring the golf pro at an open-to-the-public skills clinic demonstration.

The cost of VIP golf varies but can run from $2000 to $25,000 a day. Some companies use VIP golf extensively and believe it is more valuable to have annual contacts with specific golf pros.

Naturally, the cost will be based on the type and length of activity and how famous the pro golfer is. Even if you can't afford Arnold Palmer, you can still reap the benefits of VIP golf. Local PGA pros (teaching or touring) are often available at a fraction of the cost of the bigger name celebrities. Playing a round or attending a skills clinic with *any* PGA pro increases the perceived value of the business golf event.

Whatever level of pro you may use, handpick them carefully. Personality is more important than a big name. The objective of the event is to provide the most positive experience for the client or employee, so you'll want a pro who will mix and mingle, make everyone feel comfortable, and place the emphasis on the guests. Skill level and name recognition are important, but it is the pro's personality and attitude that will make or break a VIP event.

Summary

Whatever your budget, there is a format of business golf available to help you reach your business objectives. The decision whether to play as a foursome, sponsor or attend a corporate outing or fund-raiser, or get involved in VIP golf is a business decision based on several variables. The basic objective is to provide a positive experience for your client or employee. You do this by carefully planning the event and also by carefully selecting the right blend of people to invite.

Some of the considerations in choosing the format are your budget, the cost of the event compared to your expected dollar outcome (cost-benefit ratio), time constraints, your guest's skill and interest level, and the message the event will communicate. When preparing the guest list, you want to consider personality and skill levels. You'll also try to structure the group so everyone sees it as a good business opportunity, as well as a good time.

The industry or profession you are in and the golf culture of your organization, as well as that of your client's organization, will also impact your decisions and determine how you can use business golf most effectively.

Doctor, Lawyer, Merchant, Chief
Who Uses Business Golf and How

When I was growing up in the Midwest, the offices of all the doctors and dentists were closed on Wednesday afternoons. My mother told me it was because that is when the doctors and dentists were all on the golf course. As a small child, I envisioned some mini-health care convention taking place, with hundreds of men in white coats talking about the best way to take out tonsils and fill teeth!

Today I realize that when health care professionals head for the course, it is not necessarily on Wednesday, they're not wearing white coats, and not all of them are men! And although there may not be the medical agenda of my childhood imagination, there very well may be some talk of tonsils and teeth.

Health care professionals probably don't use golf to prospect for clients (patients) the way some other professions do. (Though there is an old story about a doctor who had his name, followed by "M.D. Hours 10 to 3," imprinted on his golf balls.) But golf does provide an opportunity to meet colleagues and to network.

Because of the many forms of business golf and many ways it can be applied to business, there is probably not an industry or profession that doesn't or couldn't use business golf in some way. Even recreational golfers sometimes play in foursomes with business golfers, so the chances are very good that if you play, you'll eventually be involved in business golf. The important question then becomes *how* you will use it. Some business people play business golf only occasionally while others use it as an integral part of their marketing and business strategy.

To get the most from this valuable business tool, you'll want to develop a business golf strategy that will parallel and compliment your career-planning efforts. Before you can do that, however, you'll want to learn as much as you can about the golf culture of your company. This, in turn, depends on how your industry, your profession, and your competition use the game. But no matter what the industry or profession, the basic question is always, "Is it worth it?"

Consider the Cost-Benefit Ratio of Using Business Golf

Whether it is an individual going out to network for a mentor or a company deciding if a golf incentive trip is the right way to motivate its sales team, the decision to use business golf is always made on the basis of what it will cost compared to the expected return. This cost-benefit ratio is then compared to the cost-benefit ratio of using other available methods to accomplish the same objective.

Look at the cost of business golf in terms of both money and time. Look at the potential benefits in terms of both short-range and long-range objectives. For example, let's say you are just beginning your career and using business golf to network. Your immediate objective is to meet and begin to develop a relationship with some high-level business executives. You hope this will eventually result in a mentor relationship that will help you develop your skills and position you to move up in your career.

Do you think it is worth spending $20 and about six hours of your time playing with strangers on a public course to try to reach these objectives? You may not find many senior-level executives on a public course. And if you are playing with strangers, it may be difficult to begin to build the kind of relationship you want. Then consider your alternatives. Do you have any friends or associates who belong to a private club? Would any be willing to invite you to play and introduce you to some of the other members? This would help you reach your objective, but at what cost? You might also consider the cost-benefit ratio of playing in a charity outing that you know a lot of executives attend. This may allow you to meet more people but on a more superficial basis. Also consider non-golf alternatives. Do the people you want to meet belong to any civic or professional organizations? What would be the cost-benefit ratio of attending a meeting?

You'll often find it is easier to quantify the cost than the benefit. It will be easier to compare the costs than to compare the benefits, since each alternative provides a different type of experience with different benefits. To help clarify the process, it is best to list the benefits in writing. You may find that for the cost, nothing can provide the benefits of business golf.

A company would look at the cost-benefit ratio of using business golf in much the same way. Usually, however, at least a portion of the benefit is quantifiable. For example, a company may offer a golf incentive trip worth $600 (the cost) to any member of the sales team who produces $300,000 worth of business (a benefit) in a particular two-month period. Or a company may invite a prospective client to play at an outing that costs the company $200 only if the business it might generate is of a certain volume, say $15,000 a year (the benefit). There may also be additional benefits, such as improved employee morale or the opportunity to break into a new market. These benefits are not easily quantifiable but could influence the final decision because they have a perceived long-term benefit.

Another intangible benefit that often carries a lot of weight in the cost-benefit ratio is trust. Many people believe that the unique nature of golf accelerates the speed at which a relationship develops and trust is born.

For some industries and professions, the benefits so outweigh the cost that business golf is almost a standard operating procedure. The cost-benefit ratio is then used to decide which form of business golf (local outing, golf vacation, hospitality tent at a pro event) will be most effective. So knowing how your industry, profession, and company use business golf is just as important as the cost-benefit ratio in developing your personal business golf strategy.

Learn the Golf Culture of Your Business

To understand the potential importance of business golf for you, look not only at your company, but also its clients, competition, and the industry as a whole. This will give you the broad picture. Also look at how people in your particular field and within your professional organizations use business golf. Tie all this into your career plan by also learning how business golf is used in the positions you aspire to in the next five, ten, and fifteen years.

You can learn the golf culture of your business in much the same way you learn the corporate culture - by paying attention, listening, talking to people, and reading. If you were asked at your initial interview if you play golf and the second or third interview was held on a golf course, you can be pretty certain business golf is important. But then you have to determine if it is important only to the company or also within the industry.

The golf culture is usually set from the top down. If the CEO enjoys golf, the chances are good that it will be used throughout the company informally and perceived as a means of breaking into the inner circle. If the CEO values *business golf*, it may be used more formally. There may be an employee golf league, team building designed around golf, and golf incentive trips and outings. If management recognizes that business golf is widely used within the industry and a critical skill in the success of the company, it may recruit and screen applicants on the basis of their interest and skill at golf, conduct employee golf clinics to encourage non-golfers to learn, and use business golf with clients and suppliers.

You can very quickly learn the golf culture of your own company by reading the company newsletter, listening to the smalltalk, and learning about employee activities. Also check the sports page for information about who is playing in local pro-ams, and the local news for information about various charity and civic outings. This will give you an idea about the golf culture of various industries and other companies.

Regardless of the golf culture of the company or industry, you will find differences in how golf is used throughout any organization based on job function. Certain departments and certain levels of employees will tend to use golf more. Even if you are in a position that doesn't encourage playing, think about how golf is used along your career track and how it may serve you in the future. Your professional organization can also give you some insight into this. Find out if the members use golf as a business tool and if a golf outing is part of the annual meeting. All this will help you decide what part business golf will play in your professional life. You'll also want to be aware of some general trends that may exist.

General Trends in How Business Golf Is Used

Certain industries and professions tend to use business golf a lot more than others, probably because experience has proven that the actual and perceived benefits far outweigh the cost. No formal survey or study has been done to determine the kinds of businesses that use business golf the most and the reasons why they do. However, the executives, golf meeting planners, and golf resort personnel that I interviewed made some interesting observations based on their own experience.

As golf continues to grow in popularity, more and more companies and organizations are planning employee meetings, conferences, and incentive trips around golf. Any industry and profession can use golf in this way and find it a valuable networking tool. Some industries, however, use golf extensively for prospect and client entertainment, while others do not. When I asked executives the reason for these trends, they usually referred to the cost-benefit ratio in an informal way: Business golf works and is worth every penny spent (the benefits are worth the cost). As I tried to dig deeper for additional reasons, many of the executives speculated and gave an opinion based on their intuition. The answers were very similar and usually related to the relationship and trust that can develop through business golf.

For example, business golf is widely used in the financial industries (banking, securities, insurance, large accounting firms). Without a tangible product, much more of the buying decision is based on the relationship between the client and the executive. As one executive put it, "What are they really buying? They're buying you. And golf provides the best opportunity to really get to know someone and develop the trust you need."

Several vivid stories I heard about the way companies in the financial industries use business golf validates this theory. A senior executive of a large accounting firm told me that when his company targets a prospective client and identifies the key individual to approach, the first question asked during the marketing strategy planning meeting is, "Does he/she golf?" If the prospective client doesn't play, the executive explained that it becomes much more difficult to develop a sales strategy. Nothing else will advance the relationship as quickly as golf can.

Because business golf is so important within the financial industry, the job interview process often includes questions about golf. Several executives also told me they were encouraged to learn the game by supervisors who understood its value. One junior-level executive was recruited by a large financial consulting firm because he played scratch golf and was on the college team. His informal job description required that he play golf two to three days a week. He was encouraged to play not only with his own clients and prospects, but also with the clients of his non-golfing colleagues! A former touring pro had a similar experience when she moved into the corporate setting with a large financial company. She quickly discovered she had been recruited more for her golf abilities and celebrity status than for her business acumen.

The travel and hospitality industries also use business golf extensively. Because these are service, rather than product-related industries, the relationship and trust developed through golf also plays a large role in the buying decision.

Manufacturers of a variety of products also use business golf for client and prospect entertainment. Although the trust issue may not be as critical when selling a tangible, the relationship between client and seller is very important in reinforcing the buying decision and getting repeat business. Business golf is the perfect way to communicate that the client is important. In a market in which competitors' products may be very similar, the relationship built through golf can be the deciding factor in the buying process. These manufacturers who focus on the importance of customer service also often use golf to strength the trust bond with existing clients.

Keeping up with the general trends and the information about your specific company and industry will help you decide exactly how to make business golf work for you.

Ideas for Developing Your Own Business Golf Career Strategy

How you use business golf and how effective it is for you depends on your profession, your industry, but most importantly, on you. Even if your company culture doesn't encourage you to play, business golf is still a valuable business skill that you'll want to have at your disposal.

A few years ago most jobs didn't require a knowledge of computers. But the individuals who were computer-literate found they were on the cutting edge. They had a very definite competitive advantage that helped them reach their career goals more quickly. Today computers are so commonplace that computer literacy is a critical and expected skill. Your career may reach a fast deadend without it.

Comparing computers to business golf may be like comparing a driver or putter to a sand wedge. You can't play the game without a driver or putter (although because of their humble beginnings, both Chi Chi Rodriguez and Seve Ballesteros learned to play without either). The sand wedge, on the other hand, isn't used as often. You can "make do" without it. But the serious golfer wants to feel comfortable and prepared for whatever comes up and therefore has a complete set of fourteen clubs.

Business golf may not be a tool that is use very often in your profession or industry. But if you are seriously career-minded, you'll want to include it in your bag of skills. Because, like the sand wedge, eventually you'll need it.

Learn the Basics of Golf as Early as You Can

Golf is a challenging game. So is business golf. If you try to learn both at the same time, you'll put yourself in a stressful situation. You wouldn't invite the boss over for dinner if you didn't know how to cook or had never entertained before. You would give yourself enough time to learn the basic skills so you would feel in control of the situation. Tackle business golf in the same way.

Practically every teaching pro I interviewed has seen an increase in the number of people taking lessons for business purposes. In some cases, the company even pays for the lessons. Several of the pros mentioned how difficult it is for someone to learn when they are under pressure to develop their game to a respectable level in a short period of time for business purposes. These individuals approach golf as a chore and miss the joy and satisfaction in the learning process. I'm sure their frustration and anxiety come across to the business associates they play with.

Take a few lessons and learn to play when the stakes are low. You may not fall in love with the game and become a serious recreational golfer. But at least you'll be comfortable and won't miss any business opportunities that involve business golf.

Many executives told me they would encourage students to fit golf into their high school or college curriculum. It can give them a life-long competitive advantage that no other sport provides.

Include a Networking Plan in Your Strategy

Golf is an excellent networking tool if used properly. It can increase your visibility and help build your reputation, both as a golfer and as a business person. Unfortunately, too many people rely on chance, just head for the course, and hope that something will serendipitously develop. It may and then again it may not. As Arnold Palmer said, "You make your own breaks - in golf, as in life." So develop a plan to make sure you get the most out of business golf networking.

Define your objective, decide how you'll reach it, and evaluate and modify your plan periodically. Be sure to keep the cost-benefit ratio in mind. And remember that one of the benefits of golf, whether recreational or business, is always **fun!**

In the section on cost-benefit ratio, I gave you a brief example of a networking plan to find a mentor. Let's look more closely at how you can develop a plan.

Before you define your business golf objective, look at your career path: where you are now and where you want to go. Decide what you need to do to get from here to there. Your long-range plan may include continuing your education to develop additional skills, joining professional organizations, and gaining more on-the-job experience by getting involved in special projects. Think about how business golf fits into the picture. This will depend on your company, the industry, and how you personally feel about golf.

In addition to looking at *what you need to know*, also look at *who you need to know*. I'm not talking about charming your way to the top without ability or manipulating people to get what you want. I'm talking about networking. If you are uncomfortable with networking, you'll find Susan RoAne's book *The Secrets of Savvy Networking* helpful.

Look at the people connected in any way to your career path: colleagues, supervisors, influential members of professional organizations, leaders in the industry, prospects, and clients. Think about each in terms of the reciprocal process of networking - how can you help them and what could they share with you. Find out if they play golf and what other activities they are involved in. Look for areas of common interest that you share with them. Then, based on the cost-benefit ratio, decide who you would like to include in your network and the best way to build that network. Decide how business golf will fit into your plan. Consider the various forms of business golf discussed in Chapter 3 and develop a plan that is right for you.

You may begin by playing with colleagues on a recreational basis. If your company sponsors an employee outing or a league, you may want to take advantage of that. Think about how civic and charity outings might fit into your plan. Don't underestimate the value of golf small talk in developing rapport. Include it in your conversation whenever appropriate.

How you choose to use golf and how large a role it will play in your career strategy is based on how you feel about the game. If you only play because it is a valuable business tool, that's okay. In that case, you'll probably use it occasionally and mostly for networking purposes. If you really enjoy it, you'll want to play whenever you can. Your skills will increase and so will your business golf opportunities as your professional relationships develop around a mutual love of the game.

Use Golf to Develop a Support System

Your network consists of all the people you know who are willing to share information with you about what and who they know. RoAne describes it as a series of overlapping circles, with the interaction between two people represented as the area of overlap. If you are not "into" golf and use it only when you have to for business, the area of overlap that is developed through golf will be very small. To enlarge the overlap and really develop the relationship, you'll have to find other areas of common interest. The larger the area of overlap, the better we know the person and the more we have in common. The larger the overlap, the more we are willing to do to help the other person and the more they are willing to do to help us.

Play golf occasionally and you can develop a network. Play on a regular basis and you'll enlarge the area of overlap and form a support system of people who will go to bat for you. They may not always agree with you about business matters, but they'll tend to be more giving because of the strength of the relationship. It's like the difference between an acquaintance and a friend.

Look at your career path in terms of a support system. Who do you want to build a strong relationship with? Can golf provide a way to do it? Executives have told me they've used golf to develop a support system that includes a mentor, members of their work team, allies from other teams and departments, members of professional organizations, and even clients. The support provided has often been instrumental in their career development. The strong nature of the relationship can also provide an opportunity to openly talk business on the golf course.

Use the Golf Course as Neutral Territory
for Informal Business Discussions

When someone is part of your support system, the relationship has developed to the point that trust exists. You both often feel comfortable casually sharing ideas about business and getting feedback off the record. The golf course can be the perfect place to do this because of the relaxing environment and the extended time frame. It is a neutral territory away from the business setting. Business discussions tend to be informal and unofficial. This gives you a great way to test out the waters without anyone losing face. Just make sure the timing is right whenever you discuss business. Read more about this in Chapter 12.

Include Business Golf With Clients in Your Strategy, if Appropriate

Your business golf career strategy may or may not involve playing with clients, depending on your particular career path. If it does, you'll want to carefully develop your strategy for prospect and client entertainment and review it frequently based on the cost-benefit ratio.

Decide If and When to Join a Private Club

As you develop your business golf strategy, one of the big decisions will always involve where to play. You have your choice of public courses, semi-private courses, resort courses, and private clubs. You'll want to find a course that will allow you to reach your objective as easily as possible (the cost-benefit ratio again). When selecting a course, consider the availability of courses in your geographic area. Also find out where the golfers in your company and industry usually play and where they entertain clients. Find out if your company holds corporate membership at a private club. And ask your local pro for information about the ratings, condition, and status of various courses.

There are many highly rated public courses throughout the country. However, in some areas, the demand is so great that it is often difficult to get a tee time. For example, 30,000 people access the telephone reservation system each weekend vying for the 2,800 starting times at Suffolk, Long Island county courses! The many public courses are also much in demand, so it's little wonder private clubs are popular with serious business golfers in this area. In some other areas of the country, business golfers have easy access to excellent public courses or resort courses, so private club membership isn't as common.

Consider what is available in your area and what is appropriate to your present objectives. Then look at your career path and think about how your needs may change in the future. Do the executives who are in the positions you aspire to belong to private clubs? If so, do you think it will be in your best interest to eventually join a private club? When? What club? What are the membership requirements?

In the past, joining a private club has been considered a good career move by many upper- middle to top-level executives. It provides an excellent networking opportunity to meet other senior-level executives, a top notch golfing environment, and a prestigious place to entertain business associates. Although the membership fee, dues, and minimum expenditure guidelines are usually costly, until recently, these costs were deductible as business expenses. It is too early to judge how the changes to the Internal Revenue Service code will affect club membership. Some club pros are speculating that many private clubs may be forced to change their membership requirements (lowering dues, allowing female members) or may decide to become semi-private courses by allowing nonmembers to play on a daily fee basis.

Get all the information you can when you first begin to think about joining a private club. Beyond the financial considerations, most clubs require that you are proposed or recommended for membership by one or more current members. Just as a club chooses new members carefully, you should choose a club with care. Some clubs are more social in nature and may even prohibit any discussion of business. Others are geared more toward the business golfer. Make sure the club you are considering does not have any restrictions that would make you or any of your business guests uncomfortable. Think about how you'll use the club and what you'll gain from membership. Again, the cost-benefit ratio will help you with your decision.

Review Your Business Golf Strategy on a Regular Basis

As you move along your career path, you'll take the time to periodically review your progress and you'll revise your plan as necessary. Also spend some time looking at how successfully you've used business golf. Review your short-term and long-term strategies and make any modifications that will allow you to use them more effectively in the future. If you think of golf as a valuable business tool, it will serve you well throughout your career.

Summary

Different professions and industries use business golf in various ways. Some use it primarily for networking, while others use it extensively for client entertainment. The decision if and how to use business golf is usually made by comparing the benefits that can be derived to the cost in

time and money. This cost-benefit ratio is then compared to the cost
-benefit ratio of any alternate methods of achieving the same business
objective. Very often business golf provides a benefit that other activities
don't: the opportunity to get to know someone well and develop a bond
of trust relatively quickly.

To use business golf most effectively, consider how it is used by your
company, industry, and profession. Then incorporate a well-thought-out
business golf strategy into your career plan.

Staying Out of the Water and Sand
How to Avoid the Biggest Mistakes
in Business Golf

"What a stupid I am." So said Roberto deVicenzo when he learned he had lost the 1968 Masters by signing an incorrect scorecard. The Argentinean birdied the 17th hole during the final round at Augusta, but his playing companion, Tommy Aaron, recorded a 4 instead of a 3. DeVicenzo signed the incorrect card. Instead of tying Bob Goalby and going into a playoff, he finished second.

Goalby earned $20,000 for winning the '68 Masters; deVicenzo won $15,000 for second place. Five thousand dollars (and a place in the record books) lost - for not knowing the score.

But how many millions are lost on the golf course *each year* - because executives don't know the score when it comes to business golf?

A golf pro at a prestigious Long Island private club told me that several years ago he saw one of the members walking back to the clubhouse after just the 3rd hole. When the pro asked what the problem was, the member angrily said, "I'm never playing with that 'blankety-blank' again, much less doing business with him. He just lost a customer worth several hundred thousand dollars a year." Mr. Blankety-Blank (the names have been changed to protect the guilty) is also a member of the club, and according to the pro, the two are still not talking. It's not just the sand traps you have to beware of out there!

Each year, thousands of business relationships are seriously damaged on the golf course. Each year, thousands of deals totaling millions of dollars are hit into the rough and lost. Later, some shrewd business deal ballhawk who knows how to avoid the mistakes of doing business on the golf course will stumble upon that lost deal, pick up on it, and then drive it home to the green.

But what are the mistakes and how can you avoid them? Some pretty savvy executives who have been very successful with business golf have shared their do's and don'ts with me. Their advice falls into six basic success "secrets" that are guaranteed to keep you out of the business golf rough.

These include:

1. Understand golf and understand business golf.
2. Define the game you are playing.
3. Set your strategy for business golf.
4. Pay attention to details.
5. Remember it is business golf. Don't slip into playing recreational golf.
6. Remember you are with a client or business associate, not a friend.

Understand Golf and Understand Business Golf

I can just hear some of you saying, "So what's to understand? I've seen enough golf on TV. I do business everyday. I'll just combine the two. What do I need to understand?" According to the experts, you need to have an appreciation for the true nature of the game of golf. You also need to know that business golf is different than recreational golf.

Golf

Mark Twain aptly described golf as "a good walk spoiled." That pretty much sums up the frustration you can feel because of the difficulty in mastering the game. But if you are going to play and use business golf successfully, you need an attitude about golf that puts the game somewhere between a pleasant experience and pure ecstasy.

The Hyatt Study surveyed over 400 top level executives who play and use business golf. Over half day-dreamed about golf during boring meetings; 55 percent said they had called in sick or left work early to play golf; 82 percent played golf in bad weather; and one in eight of these executives felt golf was more important to them than sex!

I'm not suggesting you have to find a 9-iron more attractive than your current love interest or that you should be willing to play in the middle of an earthquake that measures 6.0 on the Richter Scale. But you do have to appreciate and at least like the true nature of golf if you want to be successful - either as a golfer or as a business golfer. You demonstrate this appreciation of the game by having patience, by knowing the rules and etiquette, and by working to develop a respectable game, even though your skill level will probably never match Arnold Palmer's.

According to the National Golf Foundation, about two million people try golf for the first time each year, many for business reasons. Within a year, two out of three of these people have given it up. As a spokesperson for the National Golf Foundation put it, when you take up golf for business reasons, you have to understand that golf is not just a new weapon, it is the game of a lifetime.

Other executives I talked with came up with the following tips for developing the right attitude about the game:

- Don't expect instant gratification.
- Enjoy the game!
- Don't feel golf is beating you.
- Enjoy the game!
- Learn what golf can do for you.
- Enjoy the game!
- Understand that a large part of the game is mental.
- Enjoy the game! (I did hear this tip that often!)
- Don't put a lot of pressure on yourself to play aggressively or well.

In summary, **be patient and enjoy the game!**

The second point to keep in mind about golf is that it is a classy game with a very refined, polite, genteel image. Etiquette is a very large part of it. I don't care if you *did* attend Miss Logan's Dance and Etiquette School when you were ten and your manners are impeccable. Golf etiquette is in a category all by itself, and it can get rather complicated.

Virtually everyone I interviewed indicated that golf etiquette is even more important than golf skill. Most people will forgive you a bad shot, but most golfers have little patience when someone lacks etiquette. The feeling is "anyone can have a bad day, but only a clod ignores the etiquette."

Ignorance of golf rules and etiquette can also cast a shadow on your character on the course and in business. Bob Legg, president of Aneuser-Busch Investment Capital Corporation, advises to "read and re-read the first three or four pages of the rule book. Play the course as you find it and the ball as it lies - anything else can be construed as cheating." Also, not knowing the rules and etiquette can give the impression that you don't care about details - on or off the golf course. So **learn the rules and etiquette** and review them periodically, even if you've been playing for years. You'll enjoy the game more and other players will enjoy *you* more.

Finally, you have to **develop your skill** to an acceptable level if you really want to understand and appreciate golf. Unless you have a certain level of competency or are taking lessons to reach that level, you won't enjoy the game and won't have the patience to stick with it. Carl Person of Steel Craft Manufacturing agrees with this. Person thought the game was a total waste of time. His introduction to golf was at a corporate outing. He was so inept on the first tee that after about fifteen swings that whiffed the ball, the other members of the foursome told him to just pick it up and throw it down the fairway! Carl has developed his golf skill greatly since then. He now not only loves the game, but also finds it a valuable business tool.

On a good day, golf is a challenging and frustrating game. Without skill, it is a killer. So whether it is golf or business golf, know that you're going to have to work at it. Take a tip from a senior vice president of one of the largest commercial banks in the country: Don't wait thirty years like he did before taking a lesson!

Now let's take a look at business golf. Because even if your golf is so good that you're ready for the pro tour, you still may not understand business golf.

Business Golf

Understanding business golf is easy. But playing business golf can become complicated if you don't understand it. The simple thing you need to know and to keep in mind is this: you are *not playing golf.* You are *playing business golf.* You are not playing a round of golf. You are playing a round of business, and golf just happens to be the vehicle. Virtually every time business is lost on the golf course, it is because someone forgot that what was taking place was business and not recreational golf.

Know what game you are playing and focus your attention accordingly. Know that business golf includes golf, but goes beyond golf. Otherwise you could end up like the golfer who got a hole-in-one on the 14th hole - but unfortunately, was playing the 12th! It is the old story of know your target and how you plan to get to it, or you could end up somewhere else. These are important enough points to rank as Success Secrets Numbers 2 and 3.

Define the Game You're Playing

Before you go into a business meeting, you usually have an agenda. Whether you do a brief mental run-through or a detailed pencil and paper mapping of your strategy, you do prepare in some way. Most successful business people do.

But many of the same people who view planning as so important for a meeting in the office will grab their clubs and head for a business meeting on the golf course without a thought to their purpose or strategy. Without defining their game, the only preliminaries that seem appropriate are a few practice swings and a few minutes on the putting green.

When you don't define your game as business golf, you can very easily forget to prepare for this business meeting that just happens to be taking place on the golf course. When you don't keep focusing on the round as a round of business golf, and on the client as a client and not a golf buddy, you can easily slip into behaviors that are not effective for doing business on the golf course.

So before you head for the course, think about what you hope to accomplish with the round of golf. What is your goal, your purpose? If there is anything even remotely connected with business in your purpose, then you've defined your game as business golf and you'll want to prepare by setting your strategy accordingly.

You may be thinking, "What do I need goals and purposes for? I'm just playing a round of golf. Why make a big deal out of it?" The reason for defining your purpose and game and setting your goals goes beyond playing business golf effectively. It is a basic characteristic that successful people use to become more effective in *all* areas of their lives. Not only does it help them become effective, but it also leads to a greater sense of satisfaction and fulfillment.

Tony Robbins tells us the way to unlimited power is to know your expected outcome and modify your efforts to ensure reaching that outcome. Stephen Covey talks about beginning with the end in mind. These are great concepts for success in business as well as every aspect of life. In *Harvey Penick's Little Red Book: Lessons and Teachings from a Lifetime in Golf,* the great golf teacher stresses the importance of identifying your target and taking dead aim. Blanchard suggests that even in recreational golf, having a purpose and goals will lead to better results and greater satisfaction.

So define your purpose and goals and that will help you define your game. If you are playing with friends and you just want to enjoy a beautiful day and work at shooting your personal best, great. Focus on that and enjoy your round of recreational golf. If you are playing with a client or business associate and you want to establish rapport or develop the relationship, you will want to think about your strategy because you're going to be playing business golf.

Important point: Once you've defined your game as business golf, it is extremely important to realize that you'll actually be playing two games out there - golf and business golf. And to be really successful, you'll be playing an inner and outer game of both!

When you play business golf, you can never stop focusing on the golf part of it, but you'll also be focusing on the business part. The trick is in finding the right blend for you, but more importantly, the right blend for the client or business associate you are with.

Some people expect that business will be done on the golf course. Others prefer to focus on the game and defer the business until later (it is still business golf because you're building rapport). The trick in being successful at business golf is in being able to read people and know when to make your move. (That is why the chapter on golf behavior is so important.)

While business golf is a good way to do business, the first business to be done on the golf course is to keep the game moving. Concentrate on playing golf and at the same time pay attention to cues from the client and allow the business to develop at its own pace, whatever pace that may be.

The main point to remember is that one of your goals will always be to establish or enhance rapport. Chuck Hogan, founder of Sports Enhancement Associates and author of *5 Days to Golfing Excellence*, really summed up the importance of finding the right blend between golf and business golf when he said, "Failure to establish rapport usually happens by going too fast. If you lose the opportunity to establish rapport, you almost never get it back." *Don't go too fast!*

Keeping in mind the importance of finding and maintaining the right blend between golf and business golf, let's look at how you can develop your business golf strategy.

Set Your Strategy for Business Golf

Just as you apply setup principles to the mechanics of golf and how you address the ball, apply setup principles to the mechanics of your business meeting on the golf course and how you address the client. This should be done prior to heading for the course and involves defining your purpose and deciding on your plan of action

How to Set Your Business Golf Strategy

Let's say you've defined your purpose (networking, rapport-building, cementing a deal, team building, or whatever). To be successful in business golf, you'll consider the following points as you set your strategy to achieve that purpose.

1. **Define your expectations.** One executive in the hospitality industry often sets the expectation of getting the contract signed on the 19th hole. If you are entertaining a prospect, the expectation may focus on earning credibility by building rapport. Based on the purpose you've set, what do *you* hope to get out of the round?

2. **Know how you can benefit the client or business associate.** It is the old law of reciprocity. If you have expectations of getting something, you have to know what you are going to give in return. In rapport-building, this can be rather easily defined. Jerry Heard, the former PGA touring pro, described his approach to VIP golf in terms of benefits to the client. Heard focused on making everyone comfortable to ensure that each golfer really had a good time. He did this by *placing the emphasis on them* and on their game.

No matter what your purpose or expectations, if you take a tip from Heard and always focus on the other person, you'll have no difficulty coming up with ways you can benefit them. The important thing to remember is that the benefit should be more than simply picking up the tab for the round. For example, you could provide a networking opportunity as an additional benefit. To do this, you might arrange a foursome to include a client and a supplier who could do business with each other. That is a real value-added that could benefit everyone!

Also remember that more complex expectations may require more preliminary preparation and a real strategy. For example, the executive in the hospitality industry who expects a signed contract may have to know exactly what can be offered, in terms of hotel accommodations, meals, flights, and so forth.

3. **Set objectives.** Again, how complex and detailed this is depends on your purpose and expectations. For rapport-building, it can be simply that everyone is having a good time (indicated by their profuse thanks and a willingness to do it again sometime). The hospitality executive's objectives were more definite: The first six holes were ice-breakers; the second six holes were for relationship building; and the last six holes were for going in for the kill (making the sale). Objectives will vary. The important thing is to have some in mind so you're more likely to reach your expectations.

4. **Know your client.** Use the same strategy you would for a business meeting in the office. If you don't know the person well, you may want to call someone who knows them better. Get a read on them - how serious they are about golf, their handicap. This will impact on who else you invite to be part of the foursome and how you'll do business. Or you may prefer to use the conversation during the round to get to know the person, so you'd go in with little preliminary preparation. In this case, having the conversation skills described in Chapter 11 becomes even more important. Decide how you want to handle this by thinking of how you would handle it if it were a meeting in the office instead of on the golf course.

5. **Know your client's company or business.** Be aware of the trends, anything that has happened since the last meeting. As with preparation for any meeting, it is always helpful to review the notes you made after the last meeting or phone conversation.

6. **Re-focus periodically.** The only way to stay on purpose and to reach your objective is to have a built-in system for evaluating how you're doing that allows you to modify your strategy as appropriate.

For example, as you are recording your score on certain holes, you can evaluate how you are doing in this round of business golf - how well you are meeting your business objectives. This is also a perfect time to evaluate how well you're blending the game of golf with the game of business golf, although you'll get subtle feedback on *that* from the client throughout the round.

Pay Attention to Details

Once you've set your strategy for the round of business golf, you'll definitely want to take care of any details that need your attention. These are the issues that were mentioned over and over again as I talked to executives and golf pros. Many are important enough to be covered in detail in other chapters. They deserve mention here because not knowing them has led to damaged relationships and lost business.

1. **Golf etiquette.** The way you behave on the course is a reflection on you as a business person and as a golfer. Know the etiquette and rules - in terms of safety issues, course maintenance issues, common courtesy, and respect for the other person's game. In short, read Chapter 7 carefully, and when you are out there, pay attention to the details.

2. **Club rules.** The biggest mistake is going to the course without calling first to learn their rules. If you are prepared, organized and know what is ahead, that sends a clear message to your client that you pay attention to details, that you are on top of it, and that you leave nothing to chance - and that's really important.

Take the time to find out about the dress code, tee time guidelines, locker room rules, and any club restrictions regarding the dining room or grill and doing business in general. Several club pros have told me that they have had the unpleasant task of having to inform a member that a guest could not play or use the dining facilities because of dress code or other restrictions. Knowing the club rules can save a lot of embarrassment - and a lot of business.

3. **Gender and diversity issues.** Not being sensitive to these issues, combined with not knowing the club rules in regard to these issues is a

major business blunder. Many private clubs still discriminate against women in terms of assigning them tee times, allowing them to play on certain days of the week, or permitting them into the grill. To avoid embarrassment and damage to the business relationship, know the club rules and choose a club where you and all your guests can feel comfortable.

Before playing business golf with clients from other cultures, find out if they have played in this country before. If not, explain in detail how everything is handled at the particular course. Also determine if they need to rent clubs and if they're familiar with golf carts. Imagine how you might feel playing in a different country and pay attention to any detail that could avoid embarrassment later.

4. **People skills.** Throughout the entire round of business golf, it is absolutely critical to pay attention to what's going on – with the game and with the other person. The biggest rapport-killer, and therefore the biggest deal-killer, is a lack of good interpersonal communication skills. Know how to read the other person by listening to what they are saying and by observing their nonverbal cues. When you know their basic business style and what type of golfer they are, you'll be better able to judge when and if to talk business. Take a tip from Mike Marchev, who for many years planned golf outings for Merrill Lynch: "Pay attention. You can learn a person's character, their interests, their likes. Then you can develop a mental strategy. A lot of people concentrate on their own game too much."

Marchev's tip not only points out the importance of paying attention to the details of the communication, but also zeroes right in on Success Secret Number 5. When you remember it is business golf, you won't be focusing so much on your game.

Remember It Is Business Golf

If you don't define your game as business golf or you don't remember this throughout the round, it is easy to slip into behaviors that could end up losing you business. Even if things are going well and you've established rapport, don't forget that this is business. Always be on your best business behavior, just as you would in an office setting.

Don't care too much about the game. Remember, it is business, not just golf. Try to play your best, but don't get caught in the trap of having to win, having to break par, or having to play your personal best. Have some serious fun, but make sure the focus never switches from business golf to recreational golf. A friend of mine became aware that he had switched over into very competitive recreational golf when his client asked, "Aren't you supposed to be playing customer golf?" This was enough to focus him back to his purpose: creating rapport with the client.

In this case, playing competitive, recreational golf wasn't helping achieve that purpose.

Here are some examples of behaviors that are deal-killers and result from caring too much about the golf itself.

1. **Criticizing and offering advice.** Most people would never think of going into a client's office and offering unsolicited advice on interior decorating or organizing an office more efficiently. But they think nothing of offering their comments, criticism, and advice on the golf course. Unless you have a PGA Tour card in your wallet identifying you as a pro, save your comments until they are asked for, and then give them on a very limited basis.

For some strange reason, everyone on the golf course is an expert on the mechanics of the game. And it is usually the case that the higher their handicap, the higher the level of expertise they're willing to share. This is probably because they've been on the receiving end of so much free advice and criticism!

A teaching pro summed up the phenomenon perfectly when he told me about a husband and wife he noticed at the driving range. What caught his attention was the thud, thud, thud of the husband's ball consistently hitting the wooden divider between the driving range stalls. In frustration, the husband said: "I sure wish I could just figure out what I'm doing wrong so I could work on correcting it." To which his wife replied: "So how come you can always figure out what *I'm* doing wrong?"

It is often easier to forgive an advice-giving spouse than a business associate. When playing business golf, beware of criticizing or offering advice.

2. **Don't brag.** It is a deal-killer and a relationship-ruiner - on and off the course. Everyone admires someone who plays well - as long as you don't rub it in their faces. Let your skill speak for itself. Which brings us to the next don't.

3. **Don't talk a better game than you play.** The advantage of golf over fishing is that you don't have to show anything to prove your success! In business, this has become a disadvantage for some. They talk a better game than they play. And they are eventually found out. Plus they are sending out the message that they tend to exaggerate - and if they'd do it about golf, maybe they'd be less than honest in business matters, too.

Sometimes the cost of talking a better game than you play is a lot higher than sending out the wrong message. Ask the young female executive whose job was on the line when she was asked to entertain some important clients on the golf course. At the job interview, she lied about knowing how to play. In a panic, she expected the local pro to teach her in a few lessons. What a painful way to learn that your Mom was right all along: honesty *is* the best policy!

4. **Don't laugh at, laugh with.** Sounds easy enough, but some pretty funny things happen to people on the golf course. Ask a college friend of mine whose job interview for a large Midwest company included a round of golf with the senior executives (yes, business golf was happening even back in the sixties!) As the CEO bent over to retrieve his ball from the cup, his toupee slid off. Sidesplitting funny? Definitely - among a group of friends, and after the fact, as my friend retold the story. But it would have been a bad decision for the other executives and the job applicant to laugh as the CEO struggled to regain and retain his dignity (and get his toupee back on straight!).

Play long enough and you'll find yourself wanting to laugh at something that it is just not good business to laugh at. Control yourself unless the person the joke is on also sees the humor in the situation. Remember it is business golf - and you could end up laughing all the way to the bank!

5. **Don't complain.** So you are having a really bad round. If you care too much about the golf and not enough about the business, this can lead to some moaning and groaning. Keep in mind, you can have a bad round and still have a good time and a good day. This is possible for some recreational golfers. It is *imperative* for all business golfers.

Remember: You can lose the round of golf and still win the round of business.

6. **Don't explain.** Avoid overdoing the "woulda, coulda, shoulda" instant replays. While we learn by analyzing what we could improve on, do most of it mentally so you don't spoil everyone else's day.

Nancy Oliver, founder of the Executive Women's Golf League, believes that women tend to correct themselves or make excuses and apologize. They think it will make it look like they know what they should have done - but it is perceived as sniveling and it certainly doesn't add anything to the day. Now I don't agree with Oliver that this is basically a female characteristic, even though I'll admit that it is definitely something I tend to do! But I do agree that it creates a negative image and sends out the wrong message.

What overexplaining really communicates to the people you are playing with is that you have a hard time dealing with errors and you focus your energies on justifying or rationalizing errors rather than on correcting them. Not a characteristic anyone would want in a business associate! So do as I *now* do: Force yourself not to explain anymore!

In addition to remembering you are playing business golf, it is also very important to keep in mind that you are with a client or business associate. Sometimes things are going so well and you've established so much rapport that you feel as though you are with a friend. It is true that friendships do sometimes grow out of business relationships. But it is still critical to follow Success Secret Number 6.

Remember You Are With a Client or Business Associate

If you keep in mind you are with a client, you won't have to worry about acting inappropriately.   A few words of caution about some common hazards that have tripped up many business golfers should be enough to keep you safely in play.

1. **Don't lose your temper.**   There is one good thing about swearing and throwing clubs when you are playing business golf. At least you'll know why you lost the business. Some of these other things are so subtle they leave you scratching your head and wondering what happened.

Your friends may put up with you losing your temper. Your clients and business associates usually won't, and if they do, your golf business handicap will go up considerably.

There seems to be some sort of mystique and a certain level of humor built up around temper tantrums and club tossing. From "Terrible-Tempered Tommy Bolt," who claims he had to teach Arnold Palmer to toss the clubs in front of him so he wouldn't have to walk back to pick them up, right down to someone you probably know (I'm assuming it is not you!), the army of club tossers is legion. It is sort of a macho thing. Thirty-nine percent of the executives in the Hyatt Study reported they had thrown a club and 14 percent claimed to have broken a club after a bad shot! The game can be frustrating and the temptation is there to lose your temper, but when it comes to business golf, you just can't afford to.

2. **Beware of the 19th hole.** Many a business deal has drowned in the drink - and I don't mean the water hazards! After playing eighteen holes with a client, the rapport may be so well established you may feel you can let your guard down. Take a minute before the 19th hole to re-focus on your purpose and objectives. You may be on the way to forming a friendship, but don't misdefine it as anything other than business. Act *and drink* accordingly.

Several executives told me that they decided not to do business with someone based on 19th hole behaviors: the other person exhibited poor judgment, drank too much, and became obnoxious.

In employee recruitment, the 19th hole is often used to determine how you'd behave socially with clients and other employees. It is the perfect opportunity to find out if you would overindulge or maintain the appropriate business image.

An executive who is a member of a community business association, experienced this type of screening process. As a job applicant, he stopped at one drink with lunch, even though the other executives kept urging him to have another. After the 19th hole, he was told that although he was qualified for the job, there had been some doubt about his abilities to entertain and keep up with several hard-drinking clients! He hadn't passed the test of proving that he could handle his liquor - but he did pass the more important test of proving he could handle himself!

The safest rule is to always remember you are with business associates. Use your best judgment, and act accordingly - and don't ever forget that there are just as many traps on the 19th hole as there are on the other eighteen!

3. **Discussing inappropriate business topics.** Most people know enough to stay away from certain hot topics like controversial issues or personal matters. But in the relaxed, informal setting of the golf course, many of these same people indulge in juicy business gossip. This can happen at any time during the round, but it is most prevalent during the 19th hole.

Always remember it is business and you are with a client. Don't say anything about your company, your co-workers, or your competition that you wouldn't say if you were meeting in the office. If in doubt, don't say it. Even if it is the truth, it is more of a bad reflection on you than on the person you are talking about, and it can definitely cost you business.

Summary

There are a lot of hazards on the way to the green. When you start a round of golf, you look at the scorecard, take note of the location of the bunkers (sand) and water hazards in relation to the green, and plan your strategy. As you play the course, you survey each hole so you are aware of the possible hazards and can plan how to avoid them. Then you focus on your target. If you focus on the hazard, chances are pretty good that is where you'll end up.

In the same way, plan your business golf strategy. Know the hazards involved and respect how they can keep you from your goal. Then stay focused on where you are going. It is absolutely guaranteed to improve your business golf! And unlike Roberto deVicenzo, you won't be heard muttering, "What a stupid I am."

Beyond Polyester And Plaid
Creating the Business Golf Image

It is a cliché but it is true. You never have a second chance to make a good first impression. In business golf, your clothes and equipment contribute a great deal to that impression. So you'll want to make sure that the message you convey and the image you project are appropriate.

Proper Dress

Golf styles have varied dramatically throughout the history of the game. In the thirties, business suits and shirts with ties were appropriate. By the sixties and seventies, polyester, plaid, and pastels where the vogue. But whatever the era or the fashion, one thing has remained the same. Golf is a genteel game with a strong sense of tradition that includes a dress code.

Dress codes may be written or tacit and vary depending on whether it is a private or public course, and they are usually strictly enforced. So if you are not dressed appropriately, you won't be allowed to play! This can ruin the day for a recreational golfer. It can ruin the deal for a business golfer. Here are some tips to ensure your business golf attire is up to par.

Don't Assume; Inquire About the Dress Code

If you are the guest, you can ask your host. Better yet, call the club and ask the pro. Also find out if there is a dress code for the dining room. Get very specific information. For example, if shorts are allowed, is there a requirement that they be no shorter than so many inches above the knee? Or if jackets are required in the dining room, does it mean jacket and tie or will a jacket with a golf shirt meet the code?

Be Conservative

After you call to find out about the dress code, it is up to you to interpret the information and wear something "appropriate" for business golf. Let's say the dress code is shirts with collars, and no jeans. This is the standard dress code for many courses (although some public courses do allow jeans and collarless shirts). It gives you a wide range of choices. For business golf, you'll want to fit in. Taking a conservative approach will help you do this.

Avoid the "polyester look", which is dated and doesn't create a quality image. Who wants to do business with someone who is outdated and doesn't look successful? Many polyester blends, however, closely resemble natural fibers and convey a more upscale image.

Don't wear clothes designed for other sports or purposes. Jogging outfits, Hawaiian beach shirts, and dress shirts may have collars, but will label you as a "non-golfer." They'll also give the impression that you don't care about details.

Be aware of looking too trendy. This is a personal call, depending on your personality and style, and the people you are playing with. Knickers may be making a comeback and may look great on Payne Stewart on the PGA tour, but what message will it send if you wear them? It could be anything from "on the cutting edge" to "confident risk taker" to "throws caution to the wind." Use your judgment and decide if something is too trendy by thinking of the reaction it will have on others.

Check the messages any logos convey. On the pro tour, the logos tell us who the corporate sponsors are and who is involved with celebrity endorsements. On the golf course, logos tell your business associates something about you. If you wear a visor that says, "Hell Raisers Saloon, 4th Annual Beer Bash," will it enhance your business image? And what would a visor with a Pebble Beach logo on it say about you? Use your judgment and look at any logos on your clothing and equipment very carefully.

Check out the golf magazines and pro shops if you are still not certain what is "in." You are sure to find a look that is right for you, right for business golf - and that's comfortable too!

Go for Comfort

Make sure your golf wardrobe fits well and will keep you comfortable in any kind of weather.

Be sure you have freedom of movement.   Don't just stand in front of a mirror when you choose your golf wardrobe. Test out what it will feel like in action. Take a few practice swings and bend over as though you were teeing up or retrieving your ball from the cup.

Comfortable clothes will make you feel comfortable, and when you look good and feel comfortable, your confidence will increase. You'll also save yourself an embarrassing moment that a friend of mine had when he heard that terrible ripping sound as he retrieved his ball and realized he had torn out the seat of his pants! Not exactly the hole-in-one he had in mind.

Be prepared to be comfortable in any weather.   Sunscreen and a visor are definitely appropriate on a sunny day. If rain is in the forecast, you may want to bring a golf umbrella (avoid the tiny, collapsible kind, which will label you as a non-golfer.) Since weather can change quickly, many golfers carry a lightweight sweater or windbreaker in their golf bag, especially in the spring and fall.

When you are prepared for the weather, you send the message that you attend to details, are a contingency planner, and can handle anything that comes your way. This is the kind of person most people like to do business with.

The Typical Wardrobe

For men, a good choice would be casual or sports slacks or long shorts (if allowed) and a shirt with a collar. Knit shirts are a favorite because they allow freedom of movement. For a neater, more traditional look, always tuck in the shirt. Make sure you have plenty of pockets for scorecard, pencil, tees, and extra balls. Complete the outfit with a visor or hat and golf shoes (more on shoes later in this chapter when I discuss equipment).

For women, slacks and shorts may or may not be permitted. Knee-length sports skirts or culottes are the traditional look and are always acceptable, as are tucked in, collared shirts. Whatever you choose, you'll also want several pockets. Add a visor or hat and shoes and you are set.

Now all you need is the right equipment!

Equipment

Although most courses have a dress code, they don't have an equipment code other than that everyone needs their own clubs and bag - no sharing. Still, your choice of equipment is even more important than your dress. Your clothing reflects your personal taste and as long as it is within the acceptable guidelines, people accept it as just that.

Your equipment choices, however, are the tools you've selected to play business golf. As such, they reflect your approach to getting a job done and have a large impact on your business image.

Selecting equipment, especially clubs, can be a confusing process because of the number of variables involved. Therefore, it is best to rely on an expert, your club pro, to help you sort through all the possibilities. Here are a few tips to help you make the correct choices.

Clubs

If you are new to golf and don't yet know if you'll like it enough to make a long-term commitment, you'll want to keep your investment in equipment to a minimum. When it comes to clubs, you can borrow, rent, or buy.

Borrowing is, of course, the least expensive way to go. But if you borrow clubs, make sure they fit the image you want to project. If clubs are available from a well-meaning friend or relative, make certain they are fairly new. When I started to play, my mother offered to give me the clubs she had used "when she was young." They looked more like they belonged in the United States Golf Association (USGA) museum than on a golf course! Old clubs can affect your game as well as your image. Because of technological advances in recent years, you'll find you play much better with newer clubs.

Also, be sure borrowed clubs are in good condition. Clean them up, if necessary. Don't borrow them if the grips are so worn that they need replacement. Again, this conveys the message that you aren't concerned with details or that you just don't care.

Make sure the clubs you borrow are gender appropriate. A tall woman can borrow men's clubs and it won't affect her game or her image. A shorter woman would find it awkward to play with men's clubs because of the length. If a man uses women's clubs, he'll have a difficult time playing because women's clubs are shorter. And he'll be sending the message that it just wasn't worth the trouble to get the right equipment.

If you can't borrow the right equipment, you may want to rent some clubs. Many pro shops have clubs you can rent. Rentals are very popular at resort areas and with travelers (business and pleasure) who don't want the inconvenience of bringing their clubs along. When at home, club rental is usually the last resort for the business golfer. As a new golfer, you may rent clubs once or twice. Then if you like the game, you'll want to consider buying your own.

When you are ready to buy a set of clubs, your first decision will be where to buy them . If you are like many new golfers, you won't want to invest a lot of money, so you'll be tempted to head for the nearest garage sale. Don't. The best place to buy clubs is from a pro - at a golf course or school.

There are several reasons to buy from a pro:

- A pro can fit the clubs to your specific needs. A good fit is very important to your game. A pro will consider such things as shaft flexibility, grip, loft, club weight, and club length based on your height. You can't get this kind of help at your local thrift shop!
- You'll want to develop a good relationship with a pro. Shopping for equipment can be a way to find a good instructor to work with. (See Chapter 8 for more on this.) Also, a club pro who can help you arrange business foursomes and introduce you to other club members can become an invaluable part of your network.
- Getting your equipment from a pro reflects the kind of business message you want to project. During a round of golf, equipment is often the topic of discussion. Your friends might think it is amusing that you got your clubs dirt cheap off the back of a truck from a guy named Lefty. Will your business associates think it is as funny and clever? Probably not.
- A pro will help you make the right choices and will stand behind the sale. If you decide to invest in more expensive equipment later on, the pro may take your old clubs in trade or may help you sell them.

Let's look at some of your possible choices in terms of buying equipment for business golf.

When you are buying clubs, you should consider that most business golfers I interviewed felt that beginners get the most for their money with a good set of used clubs rather than a less expensive set of new clubs. A quality set, even used, presents a quality image.

They also believed it was preferable to start with a full set of used clubs rather than a starter set (less than fourteen clubs) that is brand new. A starter set says you are just getting into the game and not sure if you are serious about it. The full set says you mean business. Even if you don't use all the clubs at first, you can grow into it, and it presents the right image.

If you decide to buy new clubs, you have several types to select from. The pro may also use this terminology in reference to used clubs you look at.

You can buy mass-produced clubs "off the shelf." Although the concept is "one size fits all," with so many makes and models available, it is often possible to find a set that's right for you. If not, the pro can alter the clubs to meet your needs.

You also can order custom-fit clubs. The pro determines your needs. Then someone skilled at club making assembles a set from component parts to give you the proper fit - sort of like buying modular furniture. You have a broader choice of components, with each one selected to your fit.

Custom-made clubs are manufactured especially for you. The pro fits you and orders the clubs. The manufacturer begins with the raw materials and creates a set of clubs just for you. Custom-made clubs are the most expensive because of the time and expertise required to produce them.

Recreational golfers usually trade up to custom-fit or custom-made clubs only after they've become seasoned players who are serious about the game and want to enhance their enjoyment by using better equipment. Some are satisfied to trade up to a better quality of mass-produced club. Your pro can help you with this decision when the time comes.

As a business golfer, you are always aware of the image you project. Your club choice can convey messages about your priorities, your status, and how you handle money. If you show up with custom-made clubs your first time out, you may be labeled as pretentious or ostentatious. If you are just starting your career, you probably don't drive a BMW. And you probably won't choose custom-made clubs. But once you are the CEO, off the shelf clubs are about as appropriate as driving an economy car. So consider your skill level and position within your organization or profession when you choose your clubs.

Whatever you choose, the pro will probably recommend getting a set rather than individual clubs. For the sake of your game and your image, follow that advice.

Some new golfers are tempted to start with a few individual clubs and add to their collection gradually, rather than buying a matched set. Veteran golfers often fill in a starter set or supplement their collection with individual clubs they hope will improve their game. Whether you are a recreational or business golfer, you'll probably play better when all your clubs are the same make and model and matched on the basis of the fit (grip, swing weight, etc.).

The legendary pro Bobby Jones created his own set by purchasing individual clubs at various times. When he retired, the clubs were tested and, amazingly, all but one matched. Jones later said that he'd had more problems with the mismatched club (an 8-iron) than with any of the others. You probably won't play as well as Bobby Jones, but you will play with more consistency and feel more connected with a matched set of clubs.

You'll also appear to be a serious business golfer. Mismatched clubs can convey that you are indecisive about making a commitment or are reluctant to allocate the resources necessary to get the job done right.

Bag

Once you've selected your clubs, you'll want to find a golf bag that is appropriate. If you borrow clubs, be sure the bag is in good shape. Showing up for business golf with a shoddy or torn bag is as bad for your image as attending an important meeting with a gravy stain on your suit.

When you buy a bag, choose a conservative color and a size no bigger than what you actually need. Bags come in many sizes and weights. Make your decision based on:

- the number of clubs you'll carry.
- whether you'll walk or use a cart, and if you walk, if you will carry your bag.
- whether you'll take your clubs when you travel. If so, you'll want a bag with a cover that you can secure.

Many business golfers eventually get two bags, a larger one suitable for travel and a small one they can use when they walk.

Balls

If you are new to golf, you'll have an easier time selecting balls if you know the terminology. Golf balls are rated according to the hardness (compression) of the ball. Compression ranges from 80 to 100. The higher the compression, the harder the ball. Although many pros favor a 100 compression ball, most recreational and business golfers use 90 compressions.

Balata balls are three-piece balls with a liquid center and are covered with balata rubber. Surlyn balls have a two-piece construction and are covered with surlyn. Because surlyn balls are more durable and roll farther, they are the choice of most amateur golfers. Both are usually sold in *sleeves* of three balls or in boxes of a dozen.

As a business golfer, avoid using crossed out balls, which are seconds with the name crossed out. They may be less expensive, but will send the message that you don't care about quality.

Experienced balls that other golfers lost are usually for sale in the pro shop. Some may be in poor condition, but some are good buys. If you are a new golfer and prone to losing balls yourself, you may want to consider these.

Several years ago colored balls were introduced. Many golfers tried them and when the novelty wore off, continued to use white balls. Most business golfers prefer the traditional, conservative look of the white ball.

Miscellaneous Equipment

In addition to your clubs, bag, and balls, you'll also need several other important pieces of equipment. These include shoes, tees, ball markers, repair tools, head covers, towel, gloves, and sunglasses.

Whether you consider them part of your wardrobe or part of your equipment, your shoes are very important. Invest in good quality shoes that fit well and are comfortable. Soft spikes are growing in popularity and some courses have made them mandatory because they cause less damage to greens and clubhouse carpeting. However, some serious golfers prefer metal cleats because they provide added stability. Choose a style according to your own taste and what is accepted in your area.

Make sure you have several tees in your pocket and an adequate supply in your bag.

Plastic ball marker discs are available in all pro shops. You can also use a dime to mark your ball, as many of the pros do. Don't use larger coins, tees, or anything else that could deflect another player's ball.

An important piece of equipment is a repair tool. Don't leave home without it. (Chapter 7 will explain why.) Inexpensive ones are available in pro shops. Gold, monogrammed repair tools are available through most golf catalogs. Avoid using a tee to repair your ball marks. It will do the job but just isn't appropriate for the business golfer.

You'll want to protect your clubs with head covers, which are available in a wide range of styles and colors. Head covers that match or are coordinated with your bag convey to others that you pay attention to details. Avoid puppet style head covers that look like gophers, teddy bears, or other animals. These are too frivolous for a serious business golfer.

A towel attached to your bag comes in handy for cleaning your equipment. Find one that is coordinated with your golf bag. Avoid anything that obviously looks like a kitchen or guest towel, and be careful of those with logos or cute sayings on them.

Many golfers wear a glove because they believe it gives them a better grip. This is a matter of personal preference and not a required piece of equipment. You may want to give it a try and see if it works for you.

Traditionally, serious golfers and the pros did not wear sunglasses while playing because the glasses block peripheral vision and create color distortion that makes it more difficult to read the greens correctly. But with advances in modern technology and the growing awareness of the dangers of ultraviolet rays, sunglasses are gaining in popularity, both on and off the pro tour. Be aware that some traditionalists may perceive that you are not a serious golfer if you wear sunglasses.

Once you've carefully selected your equipment, treat it with care, as you would any important piece of business equipment. Never put your clubs or balls away dirty. Also clean the bottom of your shoes after each round, and keep them polished if they are leather. Keep your towel reasonably clean. How you care for your equipment says as much about you as the equipment you select.

Summary

It is just as important to dress for success on the golf course as it is in the office. Your golf wardrobe should be appropriate, comfortable, and meet the dress code requirements of the course you are playing.

Your choice of equipment can also make or break the image you want to project. A club pro can simplify the selection process for you and help you select equipment that will enhance your game as well as your image.

Now you look the part of a successful business golfer. The next step is acting the part. That begins with knowing the etiquette of the game.

Beyond Looking the Part
Etiquette

The story is told that J.C. Penney, founder of the retail chain, would not hire anyone for a management position unless he had lunch with the individual first. If an applicant salted the food before tasting it, that person was out of the running for the job. Penney believed that this minor breach in etiquette showed a tendency to form judgments and make decisions out of habit and without the benefit of all the available data.

Knowing the rules of golf etiquette can be as important to the business golfer as knowing social etiquette was to a J.C. Penney hopeful. In business golf, how you handle the golf ball is not nearly as important as how you handle yourself. Most golfers will forgive you for playing poorly. Very few will forgive you for poor etiquette. The opinions others form about you based on your poor golf etiquette strongly influences the way they perceive you as a business person.

Every golfer knows that mastering the game is difficult. But mastering the etiquette of the game should be easy. As Hilka Klinkenberg of Etiquette International told me, etiquette is just courtesy and common sense. But like common sense, it is really not that common. In my interviews, the complaints I heard most often about new golfers concerned etiquette. The majority of executives said the one piece of advice they would give any business golfer is to "know the etiquette. "

Maybe poor etiquette on the golf course is so common because there are really several kinds of etiquette involved. As a business golfer, you must know the difference between social etiquette, which in the American culture is based on chivalry, and business etiquette, which is based on the militaristic model of rank and status. You must know golf etiquette, which is based on safety issues, environmental concerns, and consideration of others. Then you must be able to apply the business etiquette to the golf etiquette and use common sense - a pretty tall order.

If you are not familiar with the ins and outs of business etiquette, you'll find Hilka's book *At Ease Professionally* very helpful. It is listed in the Resource Section of this book, along with books on golf etiquette to help you if you are brand new to the game. This chapter is an overview to put golf etiquette in the perspective of common sense and courtesy and see how it is related to business etiquette.

Golf Etiquette

Golf etiquette begins to look more like common sense and less like a lot of rules to memorize when you consider the rationale behind the rules. I find it helpful to look at the rules in terms of safety, course maintenance, and consideration of others.

Safety

Because golf clubs and golf balls can be lethal weapons, safety is always a primary concern on the golf course and at the practice range. Safety is a two-person responsibility. As the person swinging the club, be aware of possible dangers. As a spectator, understand that it is your safety at stake. Respect that the golfer's focus is on setup and swing and don't make the need to worry about your location a distraction. Keep in mind:

- When someone is teeing up, stand outside the markers. Never stand behind them.
- Don't tee off until the foursome ahead of you is out of range (usually after they've all hit their second shot). If you miscalculate and see your ball may hit someone, yell "Fore. "
- Pick up your tee before you leave. If the mower hits it, the groundskeeper could be injured or the equipment could be damaged.
- On the fairway, the player who is away (farthest from the hole) is the first to play. When another player is addressing the ball, stand still and out of range and watch the ball.
- When taking practice swings, make sure you are positioned so your divots can't hit anyone.
- After everyone putts out, leave the green together. This avoids confusion in letting the foursome behind you know that it is safe to continue play.

If you use an electric cart, be sure you know how to use it safely. Because of the terrain on a golf course, speed, sharp turns, and sudden stops can be very dangerous. Practically every club pro could tell you a story about some kind of accident involving a cart. To play it safe, you should:

- Make sure the person driving the electric cart knows how to operate it safely.
- If you've never driven a cart, get to the course extra early and have the club pro explain the basics to you.
- Know the course rules regarding cart operation.
- Stay on the cart paths whenever possible and follow the signs. They are there for your safety.

Course Maintenance

Ask most golfers why they enjoy the game so much and they'll probably tell you that, among other things, it gives them a chance to experience nature in a beautiful setting. But many of these same golfers don't seem to realize that maintaining that beautiful setting is partly their responsibility.

By mid-season, the beauty of many courses (especially public ones) is marred by holes in the fairway and circles of dead grass on the green. This could be avoided if more golfers were aware of the etiquette involving course maintenance.

On the fairway, replace divots - your own and any others you come across. If you are using an electric cart, check for sand and a shovel in the back and use these in divot repair.

In bunkers, always enter and exit a bunker from the low side. Using the high side will damage the rim and could result in an injury to you.

The rules against grounding your ball in the bunker (two penalty strokes) and taking practice swings into the sand are designed to protect the course and keep the sand in the bunker.

Always rake your footprints and marks after you play out of the bunker. This is done not so much for aesthetics but out of consideration for other golfers. Would you want to have to hit out of someone else's marks?

Leave the rake face down (for safety) by the side of the bunker (courtesy).

On the greens, pick up your feet. Dragging your feet in spiked shoes can cause a lot of damage.

Repair your ball mark. Notice where your ball hit the green and repair the small indentation it made on impact. Use a ball mark repair tool or a tee to gently lift the depression and then tap it down carefully with your putter. It is easy to forget to do this if your ball rolled a distance after it hit. But if you don't repair your ball mark, within a few days the depression will turn brown and remain that way for weeks, which will really spoil the quality of the green.

Take a tip from a high school golf coach I know, who teaches his students to repair their own and two other ball marks. That would help keep the greens in good condition and would also show you are a concerned, serious golfer.

Leave your clubs from the previous shot on the fringe of the green. Placing them on the green can also cause a depression.

If you are tending the flagstick, don't jab it into the ground when you remove it from the hole. The green is the most fragile area of the course and should be respected as such.

As you are waiting for others to putt out, don't take practice swings with other clubs. Don't risk any divots on the green!

Pick your ball out of the cup. Never use your putter to fling the ball into the air so you can catch it! The rim of the cup is very fragile and easily damaged. For this same reason, be very careful to replace the flagstick straight up rather than leaning it against the rim.

Electric carts can cause considerable damage, especially after a rain. Steer clear of all casual water and any area that is under repair.

Stay on the cart paths whenever possible.

Never drive an electric cart up to or on the green. Bags and pull carts should also be left on the side of the green.

Consideration of Others

The etiquette regarding safety and course maintenance is based mostly on common sense. The remaining rules of etiquette are based on courtesy as well. These rules are important for any player because they help ensure that everyone will enjoy the game. They are critical for the business golfer, whose primary objective is always establishing rapport and building relationships. Nothing can damage a relationship as quickly as poor etiquette that communicates you really don't care about others.

The complaints I've heard about inconsiderate golfers tend to fall into three categories: they don't know the rules; they slow down play; and they impair others' chances of playing well. Would you want to do business with this kind of golfer? What do these characteristics say about how these golfers might conduct their business?

Get off to a good start in business golf by knowing the etiquette so well that it is second nature to you. It will take some time and some thought at first, but it is well worth the effort. Don't let lack of consideration for others become your business golf handicap!

1. **Know the rules.** The USGA publishes *The USGA Rules of Golf*, as well as a "Golf Rules in Brief" pamphlet. These are available at many bookstores, most pro shops, and through the USGA (see Resource Section). Read the rules, carry them in your golf bag, and review them periodically. If you are a new golfer, you'll find the pamphlet most helpful.

The rules strictly apply in all tournament play. In recreational golf, they are applied more loosely, depending on the players. Serious golfers tend to play by the rules; new golfers are usually allowed to bend the rules a little more.

As a business golfer, your goal should be to become competent in the athletic skills of golf so that you can play by the rules. When you don't play by the rules, it can be perceived as cheating and can cast doubt on your business character as well. So before the first tee, find out where everyone stands in terms of the rules.

You can casually do this in several ways. Golfers with low handicaps are more likely to play strictly by the rules, so find out everyone's handicap before the round begins. You'll need this information anyway to determine scores. A discussion of the rules may come up if anyone in the foursome has a high handicap or doesn't have a handicap because they are so new to the game. Reviewing your rules pamphlet or asking if anyone plays winter rules (moving the ball to a better position) can also prompt a discussion of the rules.

You can communicate that you are not skilled by letting the others know that you may pick up (your ball and call it quits on a particular hole) if you are not playing well. Serious golfers will appreciate this because they'll know you don't want to slow down the game.

Knowing the official rules is only part of the etiquette. The more important etiquette issue is making sure that everyone is in agreement about the rules for this particular round, and that may involve bending the official rules. This is often done in the interest of speeding up play.

2. **Keep up the pace.** The biggest breach of golf etiquette and the one thing that will alienate you faster than any other is slow play. This is such an issue in recreational golf and creates such a back up on courses that *Golf Magazine* and the PGA have a campaign to eliminate slow play. Look for their "Pick Up the Pace" poster at your course and review the tips each time you play. Also check out slow play tips that are regularly offered in various golf magazines.

In the interest of keeping up the pace, some of these etiquette guidelines override the regular rules of the game. Know the regular rules, know the etiquette regarding speed of play, and use common sense to decide how to handle a particular situation. Indecision can slow play, so it is important to be so familiar with the etiquette that you'll automatically know what to do.

Follow these simple guidelines and even as a beginner you won't be guilty of slow play.

When starting to play:

- Pick a course that is within the skill range of everyone in your foursome. See Chapter 9 for more information on how to do this.
- Arrive early and encourage the other members of your foursome to do the same. Determine who has the honor of teeing off first, choose teams, decide on side games and wagers (if any), and identify everyone's ball brand and number *before* you get to the first tee.
- Be prepared. Get a scorecard and review it and have a pencil. Also have extra balls and tees in your pocket. To avoid confusion later, make sure none of your balls have the same brand and number (in case you use a provisional ball), and mark them, if possible. Also, always have enough money with you to cover any wagers.
- Pick the tee marker that matches your skill level: red usually designates the ladies' tees; white is for the average golfer; and blue, the advanced player. If you make the wrong choice, correct it on the second tee.
- Limit your practice swings. Take them as you are waiting for the foursome ahead of you to get out of range.
- Avoid taking Mulligans (do-overs). If the others in your foursome invite you to take one because your shot was so bad, do it quickly and only once.

To speed play throughout the round:

- Visually track everyone's ball, not just your own. When a ball is headed for the rough, use a reference point (tree, distance marker, bunker) to identify where to look for it.
- Help others if they are having trouble finding a lost ball, but limit the search to five minutes.
- Have your club for the next shot selected prior to approaching the ball. If you are using an electric cart and don't know which club you'll use, take several with you.
- Whoever is ready first should play, even though the regular rules of etiquette call for the person who is away to play first. This is called "ready golf."
- Use common sense to determine who has the honor on each tee. Usually the person who had the lowest number of strokes on the

last hole has the honor. To speed up play, your foursome may decide to give the honor to whomever is ready first. Or the honor can go to the person who hits the ball the shortest distance (you won't have to wait for the foursome ahead of you to move so far down the fairway).

- Don't be indecisive about who plays first because this can be an annoying time waster. Usually no one gets upset if you play out of turn, especially if you've all decided beforehand to play ready golf. Just be certain you don't risk hitting anyone.
- If you are holding up the foursome behind you, offer to let them play through.
- Always pull the electric cart up so you don't have to walk back for it.

To keep up the pace on the green:

- The player closest to the pin tends the flagstick, while the others repair their ball marks and prepare to putt.
- Read the break (the contour of the green) and line up your putt quickly. You are not on the PGA tour where a lot of money is riding on each shot, so don't make a production out of reading the green.
- Don't mark your ball unless it is obviously in someone's way or someone asks you to.
- If you are playing ready golf instead of having the person who is away play first, you'll also probably replace taking turns putting with continuous putting. This means once you begin putting, you continue until you putt out.
- Offer "gimmes" on putts that are so close to the hole that it is assumed the golfer will hole out. But don't take a gimme unless it is offered to you.
- The first person to putt out retrieves and replaces the flagstick after the last person putts out.
- Don't record your score until you are off the green. The foursome behind you will appreciate this.

Always be aware of the need to keep up the pace of the game and use common sense to help speed things up. Also be aware of how your behavior can affect how well someone else plays.

3. **Enhance others' chances of playing well.** Veteran golfer or new golfer, recreational golfer or business golfer - everyone wants to play well.

If your behavior lessens someone's chances of doing their best, you are not going to be very popular. You'll be perceived by everyone as either ignorant or inconsiderate. Not the business golf image you want to project. Therefore, these etiquette guidelines are extremely important.

Ironically, these are also the etiquette issues that are very often breached. I believe that is because the rationale for the guidelines isn't as apparent and it is not as easy to rely on common sense. At least that was my personal experience.

When I first took golf lessons, the instructor focused on the athletic skill and didn't cover etiquette at all. My first time out I played with a good friend and experienced golfer named Hogan (Don, not Ben!) who pointed out that I had stepped on his putting line. From his reaction, I knew it was a big breach of etiquette, but it didn't make sense to me except to confirm my belief that golfers were eccentric and golf had some pretty weird rules. It was only when I took lessons from someone who explained the rules and etiquette that I had the "aha" experience of understanding that I had actually jeopardized Hogan's chances of making his putt that day!

I find that empathizing with the other person makes these rules seem more like common sense. Just respect the other person's need to concentrate and focus on the game, and don't do anything to the course or with the equipment that might have a negative effect on how others play.

These guidelines will help enhance others' chances of hitting a good tee shot.

- Be aware that this can be the most nerve-racking shot of the game, so don't do anything to disturb the concentration of the foursome ahead of you.
- Don't crowd the first tee. Wait on the practice green until about ten minutes before your tee time, then move quickly to the first tee so you are not guilty of slowing the pace.

To help others play their best throughout the round:

- Don't create noise distractions such as talking or jingling the contents of your pockets when anyone is preparing to swing. Also don't take practice swings at that time because you'll risk being a visual distraction.
- Don't offer advice or lengthy comments on how others play or warnings about the hazards of the course. "Back-seat driving" can really influence another golfer's mental game and can ruin the

round, so avoid it. Asking what club someone used can have the same effect.

- Don't second guess *yourself.* Save the instant replay and analysis for the 19th hole. Your complaints and instant replays can break someone else's concentration, as well as affect your own mental game.
- Don't let the game get the best of you. Temper tantrums are a distraction to everyone.
- If you find another ball while looking for the one you lost, don't assume it is permanently lost and claim it. It may have ended up in the rough as the result of an errant shot on another fairway. As the old joke says, the easiest way to meet new people on the golf course is to pick up the wrong ball - but you really don't want to meet them that way! Instead, note the brand and number of the ball and share this information if you see anyone heading in that direction. You'll earn a golf star instead of a black mark!

Remembering these tips on the green will help others putt their best:

- As mentioned earlier, don't step on anyone's putting line (the line from the ball to the hole). Your footprints (especially spiked ones) create a depression on the green that can deflect the ball off the putting line.
- Don't let your shadow fall on anyone's putting line. Shadows can be distracting.
- If you are tending the flagstick (pin), ask first if the golfer who is putting wants it attended. Some golfers find the flagstick helpful in lining up their putt, in which case you remove it after the ball is struck. Do so quickly, because your fellow golfer won't be too happy if the ball hits the stick (a two-stroke penalty). If no one wants the pin attended, remove it and place it out of the way.
- When tending the flagstick on a windy day, hold the flag so its flapping isn't a noisy distraction. Also avoid creating a visual distraction by making sure your shadow and the shadow from the pin are on the same side on the hole.
- Mark your ball only if you think it is in anyone's way or if you are asked to do so (there is a two-stroke penalty for hitting another ball on the green). When marking your ball, place your ball marker right behind your ball and then pick up the ball. Later, replace the ball before you remove the marker. Doing otherwise makes it difficult to know exactly where the ball should be and may give you an unfair advantage.

- In the interest of keeping up the pace, invite someone to take a gimme if the putt is so short it is obviously impossible to miss. A gimme assumes the putt would be made and saves time because you record one stroke rather than actually hitting the ball. If it is not so obviously a gimme, extending the invitation can cause the person to feel rushed and can really affect their mental game. This is a judgment call. Use common sense.
- Don't talk about scores on the green. Asking if someone is going for a birdie or an eagle can throw their mental game off enough that they miss the putt.
- Don't record scores while someone is still putting. It can make them feel rushed and can throw off their game.
- Leave the green together. You read this before because it is a safety tip to let the group behind you know it is safe to proceed. It is also the polite thing to do so the last person to putt and the person replacing the flagstick don't feel pressured to hurry and catch up.

Thinking of golf etiquette in terms of safety, course maintenance, and consideration of others makes it a little easier to understand and remember the rules. But these are just the basics. When you have the chance, read more about golf etiquette in books and golf magazines. Your time investment will pay off on the golf course, whether you are playing business golf or recreational golf. If you are playing business golf, you'll also want to be familiar with business golf etiquette, which blends golf etiquette with business etiquette.

Business Golf Etiquette

When you are having dinner with your boss or a client, you bring rank and status-based business etiquette from the office to a social setting and combine it with social etiquette. In the same way, when you play business golf, you combine golf etiquette with business etiquette. As always, common sense and courtesy prevail, but with the added ingredient of an ever-present awareness that this is business and in business, rank and status are important.

In addition to having a good working knowledge of business etiquette and golf etiquette, there are some business golf etiquette issues to also be aware of.

Discuss Business Only If and When it is Appropriate

Deciding if and when to talk business can be the toughest part of business golf. Asking yourself the following questions will help you reach the right decision.

- Does the club allow business talk? Some private clubs have a formal policy against any type of business discussion (it is written in the by-laws and often posted in the pro shop). If you are not certain about this, call the head pro *before* you arrive for the round. That way you can plan your strategy accordingly and avoid any last-minute surprises or embarrassing situations. If the club does have a "no business" policy, you can still play business golf, but with the single objective of developing rapport and building the relationship through strictly social interaction.
- How serious a golfer is your client or boss? Again, find out beforehand so you can plan your strategy. As a rule, the more serious golfers will want to focus on the game and not discuss business.
- What is your relationship with your client or boss? In a new relationship, your primary focus is establishing rapport and building the relationship. Discussing business prematurely could do serious damage. In a long-standing relationship, you are always focusing on maintaining or enhancing the rapport. Talking business at the wrong time could create a strain, but probably wouldn't be as damaging. Before you discuss business, ask yourself how it will affect the relationship.
- What kind of signals are you picking up from the person during the round? Actively listen, be alert to what is said as well as what isn't said, and be aware of body language. This can help you decide if you need to modify your strategy regarding discussing business.

Everyone I interviewed agreed that the biggest breach of business golf etiquette is discussing business when it is inappropriate to do so. Beyond that, there were several points of view.

- Some successful business golfers believe you should never discuss business on the golf course, period. They wait until the follow-up meeting or phone call to bring it up.
- Others suggest waiting until the 19th hole.
- Some will wait for the client or boss to bring it up. This can be during the round or the 19th hole.
- Others will bring it up if the client or boss has moved the conversation into a business related area.
- And some will move the conversation into a business-related area themselves, carefully reading the feedback they're getting to decide whether or not to move into the business discussion.

All agree it is bad for business to bring it up too soon and suggest that new golfers take a conservative approach when in doubt.

Ensure That Everyone Has a Good Time

If golf etiquette is based on consideration of others and business etiquette is based on rank and status, business golf etiquette is based on having consideration for all but having the most for those with rank and status. Many of the suggestions in Chapter 9 on how to be a good host or guest are really about this etiquette issue, so read that chapter carefully. Also keep the following in mind:

- Etiquette rules concerning safety, course maintenance, and speed of play are in everyone's best interest and are usually not broken. You may, however, want to make accommodations if you are with someone of high rank and status. For example, if you are hosting the president or CEO of a company, you may want to arrange for caddies (who will repair divots and ball marks, search for lost balls, etc.).
- Be especially considerate of the person with rank and status (the boss or client). You can do this is several ways.
  1. Make certain the client is familiar and comfortable with the course (see Chapter 9 for tips on how to do this).
  2. Offer to drive the cart.
  3. Depending on the people in your foursome, the discussion on rules, honors, side games and wagering is usually deferred to the person with rank and status, who may make a decision or suggest it be decided as usual.
  4. If you have a low handicap, tailor your game to ensure the client's good time. If the client enjoys a competitive match, you'll focus more on playing your personal best. If you sense the client has a need to win, you'll probably play less competitively and focus more on relationship building. See Chapter 15 on Ethical Considerations for more on "customer golf".
  5. Before you bring a beeper or cellular phone with you (assuming it is not against club rules to do so), think of what this will communicate to your client or boss about you and your attitude toward them. If the meeting were held in an office, would you ask your secretary to hold all calls? What would be the impact of your beeper going off just as an important client who is a serious golfer is making an important putt? Ask yourself these kinds of questions and you'll be able to decide if you want to leave the equipment behind. When you do bring it along, use the phone discreetly, so you don't distract anyone or slow down play.

These tips will help guarantee that everyone enjoys the round. They'll also help you project a positive image as a competent, considerate business golfer.

Always be Aware of the Image You Are Projecting

People tend to do business with people they know and like and perceive as being similar to themselves. This fact is the reason networking is so popular and such a valuable business tool. It is also the rationale behind using golf as a business tool. A round of golf provides ample opportunity for others to get to know you. Use good golf etiquette and common sense to make sure that the you they get to know is someone they like and regard as a kindred spirit.

Focus on being considerate and outer-directed. You'll create the image of someone who is confident and competent, and you'll gain respect. Don't fawn over others or use excessive flattery. You may be perceived as an apple polisher.

Rapport can be built and relationships developed very quickly during a round of golf. Keep in mind that it is still business and continue to respect rank and status no matter how friendly things get. Be aware of body language and always respect the other person's space. A slap on the back or high five may be appropriate when a friend makes a good shot, but not when a business associate does the same. Also be careful of casual comments that may not be appropriate.

Adapt your approach to golf to more closely match the other person's. If they are really serious about the game and you are just out to smell the roses, it will be more difficult to build rapport. The same holds true if it is their first time out and you are a serious golfer. Try to see things from the other person's perspective. The more the other person perceives you have in common, the easier it is to build the relationship, and the more they will tend to like you. This isn't manipulative. It is the same as preparing something special, bringing out your best china, and using your best table manners for company.

Be especially aware on the 19th hole where you shift from golf etiquette to social etiquette. Continue to use business etiquette and don't fall into thinking it is strictly a social situation.

Summary

Good etiquette is critical to success in business golf because how others perceive you on the golf course strongly influences the impression they form of you as a business person. As a business golfer, you need to have a solid working knowledge of golf etiquette, business etiquette, and business golf etiquette. All three are based on courtesy and common sense. Business golf etiquette, like business etiquette, also focuses on rank and status.

Even though etiquette is more important than athletic skill, you'll still want to work to improve your game. This will make you feel more comfortable about playing with golfers of all skill levels. Your initial goal should be to develop a respectable game (100 to 115), so others look forward to and enjoy playing with you. If you excel and become a low handicap or scratch golfer, congratulations! It can gain you a big advantage in business golf.

Getting in the Swing
Golf Skills

If you are going to play business golf, you have to know how to play golf - and it can be a difficult game to master. Baseball great Henry Aaron captured the frustration of it when he said it took him seventeen years to get 3,000 hits in baseball, but he did it in one afternoon on the golf course. Though I'm sure Hank Aaron exaggerated his score for the round, he was on target in identifying golf as a game that can humble even the greatest athletes. But with an understanding of the fundamentals, consistent practice, and a commitment to learn, it is possible to develop a skill level that will allow you to feel comfortable playing with anyone - even business associates! Of course, the better your skill level, the more comfortable you'll feel.

Have I suddenly changed my belief that etiquette is more important than skill level? Not at all. Let's look more closely at the two and put the relative importance of etiquette and skill in proper perspective.

Ask most golfers which is more important and they'll probably say etiquette. This is because your poor etiquette will affect their game more than your lack of skill will. Therefore, they'll forgive your low skill level more easily than they'll forgive your lack of etiquette. But ask them who they would rather play with and they'll probably tell you someone who has both good etiquette *and* a decent skill level.

Look at it in terms of what etiquette and skill level communicate to others about you and the picture becomes more complex. If you have a low skill level, it means just that - you don't play well. The reason could be you are new to the game or don't play very often. Whatever the reason, people don't usually take it personally or get upset, because they know how difficult it can be to play well.

If you don't use proper etiquette, much more is communicated about you. Because etiquette is so much easier to learn, poor etiquette tells the other person you don't care enough about the game or about them to bother to learn. It labels you as inconsiderate. This negative opinion tends to be generalized, which is what psychologists call the "horns effect." So others think if you behave this badly on the golf course, you must behave just as badly in social and business situations too.

A poor skill level doesn't carry this horns effect. However, as you develop your skill level and become a capable golfer, you'll often find that the halo effect, which generalizes a positive opinion, is at work. Some people will assume that because you are a good golfer, you are also good at your job. Many of the women I interviewed told me that they had impressed certain people as capable golfers and that this had a direct impact on how they were perceived in business. Because of their golf skill, they didn't have to work as hard to establish their credibility in business.

The conclusion is that good etiquette is necessary to *maintain* your positive image, and a good skill level is desirable because it can *enhance* your positive image. Playing a respectable game will also go a long way in building your confidence - a quality you definitely want to convey in business golf. So seriously focus on developing your game to become a proficient business golfer.

The purpose of this chapter is not to teach you the technical skills of golf, but to help you find a way to learn the skills you'll need to feel comfortable playing business golf. I've tried to simplify the learning process so the new business golfer can cut through the huge body of contradictory information that exists. The basic process applies to veteran golfers as well as those brand new to the game: Find an easy way to become proficient.

Learn the Game

Notice I didn't say, "take lessons." There are a lot of ways to learn to play golf. Some excellent golfers have never had lessons but have picked up the skills along the way. Many start at the driving range, then read books, watch videos, subscribe to golf magazines, watch the pros on TV and listen to and watch others in their foursome.

Use whatever method is best for you. But be aware that there is a lot of conflicting information out there and it can get pretty confusing. It can also take longer to learn by this kind of trial-and-error method. Books and videos can't give you the one-on-one attention and feedback that you get when you take lessons. Even veteran golfers find they can improve their game with a few lessons.

Before you take lessons, give some thought to the type of experience you are looking for and the level of commitment (money and time) you are willing to make. Your decision will be based on your objective - whether you are interested in business golf or also want to become a serious recreational golfer. In either case, the points you'll want to consider remain the same.

Group Lessons versus Private Lessons

If you are just starting out and haven't really made a commitment to the game but want to learn more, you'll probably want to consider group lessons. There are many advantages, including:

- The cost is lower. Lessons offered through your local high school, college, adult education, Y, driving range, or public course aren't nearly as expensive as a series of private lessons would be.
- More relaxed atmosphere. Because the instructor's time is divided among several students, there is less pressure on you to perform. This also gives you time to practice while the instructor is working with others.
- Networking opportunities. A lot of new golfers don't stay with the game because they don't have anyone of their own skill level to play with. Taking group lessons will introduce you to many new golfers and this can help you get involved more quickly.
- High schools, colleges, and adult education classes are often conducted by teachers or coaches who are skilled in both golf and instructional methods. This makes it easier for them to adapt their teaching style to your particular needs.

Because of these advantages, group lessons are a great way to test your interest in golf without making a big commitment. Many people begin with group lessons, find they enjoy the game, and move on to private lessons. Although private lessons do cost more, they also have some advantages. These include:

- Individualized attention. The instructor works one-on-one with you throughout the lesson, so it is less likely you'll pick up bad habits.
- The lessons are specifically tailored to your needs, so you can target a particular skill to work on. Many experienced golfers will take one or two lessons to correct a problem they are having with a particular shot.
- Private lessons are often videotaped. Watching yourself and having the video to review can be an extremely valuable experience.

After you've developed some skill and are committed to learning more, you may want to attend a golf school. If there are none located in your area, check the ads in any golf magazine for more information. But be aware that the format is very intensive and can be a turn off to newcomers.

Finding the Instructor Who is Right for You

Whether you decide on group or private lessons, you'll want to find an instructor who will help you reach your goal as quickly and painlessly as possible. The greater your commitment to learning the game, the more important it becomes to make sure you and your instructor are on the same wavelength. You can get information to help with your decision by reading the course description for group lessons or by talking with the instructor. There are several things to consider, including basic compatibility, the teacher's skill level, and the method of instruction.

Is the instructor a person you feel good working with? You don't have to be totally compatible in personality or temperament, but you should get a feeling that you can learn from this person. You should also be willing to make a commitment to give the instructor's ideas a chance to work before you run out and buy yet another video or book with suggestions that conflict with the instructor's.

You also need to consider the instructor's skill level. It is a talent and skill to know how to play well. It is a different talent and skill to know how to teach someone else to play. Be sure the person who is teaching you has both skills.

A degree in education or a background in teaching is not necessary (though many LPGA pros have these credentials). The PGA and LPGA offer seminars on instructional methods to their teaching pros, so there are many capable teachers out there. The important question is: Can the person you are considering teach you?

Too often beginners are totally confused after their first lesson or two and either blame the game for being so complicated or, worse yet, blame themselves. True, there is a lot to learn. But the instructor's job is to find a way to communicate what you need to know in a way that you can understand and apply. This requires an instructor with a lot of patience, flexibility, and good communication skills. The easiest way to find this out is to talk with the instructor about what the lessons include and how the information is presented. If you are considering private lessons, you'll also want to know that the instructor is interested in your needs and is willing to tailor the lessons for you.

The method of instruction is also important. Does the instructor follow a teaching model of explaining, demonstrating, observing you, and giving you feedback during each step of the learning process?

In what sequence will you learn? Many instructors today focus first on the short game (putting chipping, pitching) because these skills are somewhat easier to learn. This is a good learning format for the business golfer because mastery of these skills can improve your score very quickly. This approach also builds your confidence about your skill level, which keeps you interested in the game.

Does the instructor recommend books or videos to facilitate your learning? Are there practice drills and exercises (beyond just hitting balls) that you can work on between lessons to help you master certain principles?

Will the instructor teach you how to set objectives and keep a record of your progress? This will help you continue developing your skill level long after the lessons are over.

The teaching methods and learning process the instructor uses are important because they are factors in how quickly and easily you'll learn. It is equally important that the lessons cover all the important topics you'll need to know. Obviously, you are taking golf lessons to learn the technical skills of using a club to hit a ball. But golf involves so much more than just technical skill - and you'll want your lessons to include more, too. You may not devote as much time to these other areas, but they should not be overlooked.

Lesson Content

Your instructor's job is to prepare you to function well on the golf course. There is no way you can do this without knowing the rules and etiquette. You may be way ahead of the game on this, but the instructor should still go through it with you.

Your lessons should also include warm-ups. Golf may not be as physically demanding as tennis or racquetball, but it is still a sport that places certain demands on your body. Make sure your instructor gives you some warm-up exercises to use before you practice or play. The warm-up exercises will limber you up so you'll play with greater flexibility. They'll also help you avoid muscle injuries.

The fun part is the technical part of the lesson - you actually get to hit the ball! It can also be the confusing and frustrating part, - because there are so many things to learn and so many different opinions about how to do it.

I believe it is important to find an instructor who'll simplify and clarify things for you by having you first look at the big picture so you'll know how all the pieces fit. Then you'll be able to listen to all the contradictory suggestions and decide what will work best for you.

If your instructor uses the technical model of laws -principles -preferences that has been around for over twenty years, you'll have a good understanding of what golf is really about. This model is discussed in a lot of the golf literature and Gary Wiren explains the model in detail in his excellent book *The PGA Manual of Golf: The Professional's Way to Play Golf* (see the Resource Section). Here is a brief look at how it works so you'll understand the basic concept.

There are five ball flight laws that determine the direction and distance the ball will travel. All five laws relate to how the clubhead meets the ball. Knowing these laws helps you understand why the ball reacts as it does and allows you to analyze your actions and self-correct. The five laws relate to:

1. Speed. The speed of the clubhead at impact largely determines the distance your ball will go.
2. Path. The direction of the arc of the clubhead (the swing) will determine the direction the ball will go.
3. Face. Direction is also determined by the position of the clubface when it hits the ball.
4. Angle of approach. The angle of the clubhead in relation to the ground will affect both distance and the trajectory of the ball.
5. Squareness of contact (the "sweet spot"). Both distance and direction are affected by how close the point of impact is to the center of the clubface.

These laws always hold true. If your ball doesn't go where you want it to, the laws will help you understand why. It is cause and effect: If you follow the laws, you'll be able to control the ball. Of course, I've just given you the basic laws. You also need to know how to analyze your shot in terms of the laws. Your instructor will do this for you at first and should gradually teach you how to do it yourself. The way you implement the laws is by using the principles.

There are also fourteen principles that influence both distance and direction. The way you execute these principles determines the position of your clubhead. As you become more familiar with the principles, your instructor should teach you how each principle affects the position of the club. This will tell you which law each principle relates to.

The first three principles are the basic skills you'll want to master first. They are grip, aim or alignment, and setup. Grip is how you hold the club. Grip has the greatest influence on clubface position. Aim or alignment is how both your body and the clubface are lined up with the target. Setup is your posture, stance, weight distribution, and the position of the ball.

The remaining principles concern such things as swing plane, the width and length of your swing arc, timing, and balance. As you gain a greater understanding of the principles, the influence they have on direction and distance, and their effect on the clubhead, you'll see your game improve dramatically. You'll also find you will develop certain preferences in how you implement the principles.

Preferences relate to personal style. Since everyone is different, there is no limit to the number of preferences. Think of how different the touring pros look when they play. They all use the principles in order to apply the flight laws. But they all have their own preferences in exactly how they implement the principles. For example, when you apply the principle of grip, you may prefer the overlapping grip or the interlocking grip. As you develop your game, you'll find a certain posture, stance, and weight distribution that feel right and work for you. These will be your preferences within the guidelines that make up the setup principle.

The many contradictory opinions you'll read about in books and golf magazines are based on personal preference. You may find that some of them work for you. But be aware that all the principles are interrelated - when you make a change in one by trying a different preference, you'll also see a change in regard to other principles.

When you are first learning, it is best to focus on the laws and three basic principles and build from there. Keep in mind that learning to play is a process, not an event. The process will be easier and clearer if you understand the role of the laws, principles, and preferences.

This model will help you master the mechanical skills of golf. But the technical skills include another ingredient that will help you play your best. This important skill is called course management and your instructor should spend some time focusing on it.

The real challenge of golf involves matching your skills to the particular course and course conditions. This involves knowing yourself, knowing the course, and planning your game accordingly. Some of the specifics of course management you'll want to learn will include:

- How to use the yardage, par listings, and course layout on the scorecard to plan your game.
- How to set your own par for the round.
- Club selection.
- How to decide whether to play cautiously or boldly.
- How to select your target and plan one shot ahead so even if you miss, your ball is still in the best place from which to play the next shot.
- How to read the green and the break of the ball.

Course management also includes a component that goes beyond technical skill and focuses on the most important six inches in golf - what's going on in your head. Make certain that your learning includes attention to the mental aspects of the game as well as to the technical skills.

Self-management is just as important in golf as the technical skills and course management. Find an instructor who appreciates the mental game of golf and can help you develop your self-management skills. This might include:

- Focusing on the importance of relaxation, initially through deep breathing and possibly later through visualizations or imagery.
- Building your confidence by focusing on your strengths, and providing positive feedback regarding corrections.
- Developing the ability to concentrate and focus on your objective rather than on overanalyzing the details.

Your mental attitude and self-management skills play a large part in determining how quickly you'll become a competent golfer. The starting point is making a commitment to learn.

Your Personal Commitment

Golf is often called the game of a lifetime. When some people say this, they mean that anyone at any age can enjoy the game. When committed golfers say it, they mean that throughout life golf continues to be a challenge and often a lifetime is not long enough to really master the game.

Whether you are a dedicated recreational golfer as well as a business golfer or strictly a business golfer, if you want to get the most out of the game, you have to make a commitment beyond just taking lessons. Your level of commitment in the following areas will determine how well you'll do and also how much you'll enjoy the game.

Practice

Depending on how much time you can devote, there are several ways to practice your golf skills. You can start with drills and exercises. Some of these don't even involve hitting a ball. For example, just a few minutes a day spent practicing your grip, aim, stance, and swing will help you get a lot more out of each lesson.

Since putting usually involves between 30 and 35 percent of the game, practicing this skill as often as possible can really pay off. Most public courses have at least one practice green. They are free and there is usually no waiting time. As little as ten or fifteen minutes practice two or three times a week can make a big difference in your putting and in your score.

When people think of practicing, they often think of hitting a bucket of balls. This can be an important part of your practice routine as long as it is structured practice. Have a definite objective in mind, know what clubs you'll work with, pick a target, work on your grip, aim, and setup, and analyze the results you get. This will help you improve your game. Slamming quickly through the bucket without a learning plan just isn't as effective.

The best way to practice all the skills involved is to play as often as possible. Practice greens and driving ranges are usually flat and don't truly represent the challenges of the game. They can also give you a false sense of confidence about your game because they don't call all the necessary skills into play.

If you are just beginning, you'll find less challenging courses such as pitch and putts, par 3's, and executive courses a good way to build your skill without becoming frustrated. If finding the time is a problem, playing nine holes in the late afternoon may be a way to keep your commitment to practice, practice, practice.

Make a Commitment to Your Teacher

As mentioned earlier, there are so many opinions about how to play because a lot of it is personal preference. When you are first learning, you'll get a lot of information about a lot of preferences from a lot of sources. This can be very confusing, especially if you still don't have a solid understanding of the laws and principles.

To avoid this confusion, make a commitment to follow your instructor's recommendations until you feel you are well grounded in the basics. Rob Gilbert, my friend and mentor, says it best in his book *Gilbert on Greatness: How Sport Psychology Can Make You a Champion*. Rob has two rules regarding coaches:

Rule Number 1: The coach is always right.
Rule Number 2: If the coach is wrong - reread Rule Number 1.

The point is that the more time you spend evaluating, comparing, and criticizing the coach or instructor, the less time, energy, and effort you spend on your own performance. So wait until you know the basics before you start shopping around for different ideas on personal preferences.

Make a Commitment to Your Mental Game and to Self - Management

Hopefully your instructor introduced you to the importance of the mental game and you really believe it is just as important as your technical game. As time permits, make a commitment to read more on the subject (see the Resource Section). At the very least, promise yourself that you'll make a conscious effort to keep a balance between taking the game seriously and stopping to smell the roses. This allows you to bring all the required skills together - the technical, mental, and physical - and still keep everything in perspective. It also helps you maintain the delicate balance between golf and business and lets you project a positive image.

Combine a challenging game and a business agenda, and stress or tension could result. So always make relaxation and enjoyment part of your agenda. Be aware of the beautiful setting. Breathe in the fresh air. Even on the practice green or driving range, flow into the experience and become part of the process. One of your goals in business golf is to make sure everyone is having a good time. This starts with you!

You also need to concentrate and focus. As you prepare for each shot, put everything else out of your mind and totally concentrate and focus on that shot. A golf coach I know suggests the following mental trigger or cue to help you achieve this focus. Just before you address the ball, tell yourself you are going to *GAS* up or that this is the *PGA*. Both are acronyms to get you focused on the three basic principles: GAS (grip, aim, and setup) or PGA (posture, which is part of setup; grip; and aim).

Go through this process before you put the ball in flight just as a pilot goes through a checklist before putting the plane in flight. Make sure of the mechanics of the three principles, but beyond that, don't overanalyze. This process helps you get so focused that your swing should just flow because it feels right. It is your intuitive right brain taking over from your analytical left brain. For more on this, you may want to read *The New Golf Mind* by Gary Wiren and Richard Coop.

After you've hit the ball, analyze the shot. Then *let it go.* Focus on other things - the people in your foursome, your business agenda, or your surroundings. Then as you approach your next shot, focus back to GAS or PGA and totally let go of whatever else you were thinking about or discussing (especially if it was business!).

This process will help you play your best, achieve your business objective, and enjoy yourself because it allows you to be in the moment and fully focused on the task at hand. To do this, you have to be aware of what is happening around you. More important, you must be aware of your thoughts - what is happening in your head. Only then will you be able to switch focus and concentrate on the moment. This is what the mental game of golf is all about. Confidence plays a big part in it.

In golf as in life, your level of confidence greatly influences your actions and the results you get. In golf as in life, it is difficult to be confident, because if you are like most people, the little voice in your head is usually giving you negative messages. It is important to be aware of this and to make a conscious effort to use positive self-talk and to screen for the positive.

In the chapter on etiquette, I didn't mention that it is rude and totally inappropriate to make negative comments about the skills of the people in your foursome. I assumed we all know that making disparaging remarks about someone else's game can really shake that person's confidence level and affect how they play. No civilized person would do that. But we do it to ourselves all the time!

That little voice in our head is very quick to give us a negative message on just about anything. The mental game of golf involves becoming aware of the messages we are giving ourselves and replacing the negatives with positive self-talk. This is especially important in business golf because it will not only influence your game, but the image you project and your confidence level about the business relationship.

Be realistic with your self-talk. You are only setting yourself up if you tell yourself you are going to hit a hole-in-one or shoot par or better on every hole. Your little voice knows better and will quickly come back with, "Oh, yeah? Who are you trying to kid? Not in a million years."

Instead, just become aware of your negative thoughts and be as kind to yourself as you'd be to someone else. Change a thought such as, "Oh, brother! In the sand again. This should be good for at least three strokes!" to something like, "Even the pros end up in the sand. This is part of the challenge of the game. I've made tougher shots than this before and I can do it again."

If you already use positive self-talk in other areas of your life, great! It will serve you well in golf because the many challenges of the game create a lot of opportunities for the negative messages to creep in. If you haven't used positive self-talk before, don't limit its use to golf. It is a wonderful tool that can truly change your life.

Positive self-talk is designed to control negative thoughts and messages that can erode your confidence and performance. There is another tool that works in the same way but with experiences or situations rather than thoughts and messages. It is called screening for the positive.

You have control over what you enter into your business computer and save. In the same way, you have control of what you program into your mind and save. While most of us know about GIGO (garbage in, garbage out) and are careful about what goes into our PCs, we are not as discriminating about our minds. In fact, we tend to hold on to the garbage (negative experiences) and refer to them more than we do the valuable, positive experiences. This is screening for the negative. The mental game of golf involves screening for the positive instead.

Earlier I suggested fully concentrating and focusing on your grip, aim, and setup; hitting the shot; analyzing it; and then letting it go and changing your focus. Let's look more closely at the analyzing and letting go part of that routine to see how you can screen for the positive.

Our normal tendency is to analyze based on the results. If the shot meets our expectations, we often let it go without much further analysis. If it wasn't up to our standards, we tend to analyze it to death and are very reluctant to let it go. The experience we'll more often store in our mental computer is the negative experience! Days, months, or years later, we are still retrieving that saved experience in the form of negative self-talk that continues to erode our self- confidence.

To screen for the positive, analyze the situation. If it is a good shot, be in that moment with all your senses. Make a conscious mental note of what you did, what it felt like, the visual image of the ball hitting your target. Then deliberately save that mental file to retrieve and use in your self-talk later on. Then move on to the next task at hand, confident that you can retrieve this experience at anytime.

If you didn't meet your expectations, analyze what you did well and what you need to focus your attention on. (Notice I didn't say, "what you didn't do well" or "what you did wrong".) Make a conscious mental note of the positives. Include an action plan for learning that will allow you to make progress toward bringing this type of shot up to your expectations. This will let you save only positive experiences. There'll be no negative experiences saved for the little voice to use in future self-talk.

Chuck Hogan's book *5 Days to Golfing Excellence* and Ken Blanchard's *Playing the Great Game of Golf* can help you develop the skill of screening for the positive. It is a skill that is shared by all high achievers - on and off the golf course. As a business golfer, you'll find making a conscious commitment to screen for the positive will help both your golf and your business.

Summary

In business golf you need a level of golf skill that allows you to feel comfortable playing with anyone and makes you a desirable part of a foursome. Quality instruction that focuses on the technical, physical, and mental parts of the game as well as on the rules and etiquette is the starting point. However, your personal commitment to develop your skill is the crucial factor.

The Front Nine of Business Golf
Playing in a Foursome

Ask anyone where golf originated and the answer you'll probably get is Scotland because that is where the format that is played today was developed. But early records show that similar games were also played in Holland, Belgium, and France - and even in Ancient Rome and China!

Although it is difficult to pinpoint the exact origins, it seems foursomes have been in vogue throughout golf's history. Documentation from as early as the thirteenth century refers to a game similar to golf that was played by teams of *four* players!

Regardless of when, where, and how the idea of foursomes developed, it is safe to say most business golf is played this way. Some team building and employee development golf activities call for larger groups, but the foursome is still the basic unit in golf. Whether you are the guest or the host, you'll want to make sure that your business golf etiquette within the foursome is up to par.

When You Are the Guest

A business associate has just asked you to get together for a round of golf. If you are a new golfer, this may generate some anxiety. You may not yet feel comfortable with the game, and the idea of playing with a business associate and having to maintain your image can be a little scary. If you've been playing a while, you may be tempted to drop everything, grab your clubs, and head for the course.

Compare your reaction to the golf invitation to how you'd behave, feel, and think if the business associate had instead asked you to get together for a meeting in the office or over dinner. Chances are pretty good that you'd give some thought to the possible business agenda and do everything you could to be a good guest. So why not follow the same modus operandi for a business meeting held on the golf course. No matter how well you play or how long you've been playing, prepare for both the round of golf and the round of business golf. To get things off to a good start, clarify the invitation. You'll avoid confusion and possible embarrassment, and feel more comfortable if you do.

Clarify the Invitation

Even before you inquire about the specifics and logistics of time and place, you'll want to be sure you understand the basics - like who is paying?

Are you a guest or are you going fifty-fifty? Listen very carefully to how the invitation is worded and don't make assumptions or leap to conclusions. Misunderstandings can occur very easily because of the way a question is asked and also because of what is going on with the listener.

For example, suppose you live in California and your business associate says, "I'm driving down to play Pebble Beach next Thursday. Would you like to join me?" It is impossible to tell from the question whether or not your associate plans to pick up the tab.

It is also the kind of question that could trigger an emotional reaction in a lot of golfers, especially if they've never played Pebble Beach. So a typical response might be, "Oh, boy, I'd love to. What time are you planning to leave here?"

Based on the nature of your relationship and how well you know your business associate, you could make an assumption about who is picking up the tab. (Also, if the invitation is to a private club and your associate is a member and you are not, that could be a clue that it is a genuine invitation.) But making an assumption is risky business - if you are wrong, it could be very awkward, embarrassing, and costly (a round at Pebble Beach, for instance, with cart and refreshments will add up to several hundred dollars). Worse, it could really damage the business relationship.

So before you accept an invitation, be sure you know the true nature of the offer. Of course you can't come right out and ask, "Who is paying?" or "Is this on you?" But you can ask "What do green fees run at Pebble Beach these days?" If the answer is something like, "Green fees are $$$ and the carts run $$," you know you are on your own. You'll be expected to pay your green fees and 50 percent of the cart rental. But if your associate says, "Oh, no. Don't worry about that. I'd like you to be my guest!", you'll have clarified the situation for yourself and maybe even given your associate a hint on how to word invitations the next time around.

After this important issue is settled, a discussion of handicaps may be appropriate, especially if you are a new golfer or if you think your lack of skill may spoil the other person's enjoyment of the round.

The handicap system was designed to keep the game interesting and competitive when people with various skill levels play together. So even if you are a brand new golfer and don't have a handicap yet, you could still play in a foursome with highly skilled golfers. This is the way the game is structured.

In the real world of business golf, we have to consider that structure in terms of individual preferences, personalities, and behaviors. The game may allow a scratch golfer to play with a duffer. That doesn't guarantee that the scratch golfer or the duffer will enjoy the round.

The Hyatt Study found that 89 percent of the executives surveyed preferred to play with people who are better golfers than they are. This may tie into the competitive nature of business executives, since 82 percent also agreed that they always try to beat the people in their foursome.

It is probably pretty safe to say that these executives wouldn't enjoy the round very much if they were in a foursome with three brand new, unskilled golfers. But what if they were with two better golfers and one newcomer? That is where individual personalities and behavioral styles come into play. Some golfers would enjoy the round very much and give the newcomer credit for wanting to learn. Others might enjoy it only if the newcomer seemed serious about it and didn't slow down the game. And some very serious golfers do not enjoy playing with unskilled golfers, *period.*

Although setting up a foursome is basically the host's responsibility, building rapport and developing the relationship are objectives that are always shared responsibilities. So you as the guest may want to give some input, especially if you are not a skilled golfer and you believe your lack of skill could spoil the round for anyone in your foursome.

If your host has at least a ballpark idea of your skill level or if you play a respectable game, the topic of handicaps probably won't come up until the foursome gets together just prior to tee time. But, if there is any possibility the host thinks you are a much better golfer than you are, clarify this at the time you receive the invitation.

Just as there is a tactful way of finding out who is paying, there is also a way to clarify your skill level without saying something like, "You've gotta be kidding. You're a great golfer and you want to play with me?" Remember this is business golf, and your image as a golfer is intertwined with your image as a business person. So don't apologize or put yourself down in any way because you are not a great golfer. Take that information and use it to your advantage, to develop rapport and enhance your image by focusing on the needs and concerns of the others. You may not be a great golfer, but this will prove that you are a great business golfer!

You can initiate the discussion by asking about the course or the others in the foursome. For example: "I've never played that course. Is it very difficult? I'm new to the game (or still struggling with the game). What do you think?" or "I love the game but it is still a real challenge for me. I can't seem to break 120. But I pick up when I reach a maximum so I don't slow down play. Do you think this will be okay with the others in the foursome?"

Handling the situation in this way brings it out in the open and avoids any problems or embarrassment later on. It also sends the message that you are the kind of person who is straightforward, able to deal with possible issues in a proactive way, and are considerate of others - exactly the kind of image you want to project.

Initiating this discussion may bring up the question of your handicap. If you don't hear it when you are invited, you'll definitely hear this question when the foursome meets the day of the round.

Calculating a handicap is complicated and is based on your recent scores, but it basically represents your average number of strokes above par. It clarifies your skill level and helps to determine where you stand in relation to other golfers. The lower your handicap, the better golfer you are.

Be sure you are familiar with the concept of handicaps. The USGA has several pamphlets on the topic and most golf books for beginners also discuss it at length (see the Resource Section). The USGA has several ways to handicap the unhandicapped, but usually a maximum of 36 is assigned for a beginner. In some tournaments, 50 is the maximum and is based on three strokes for each hole except for the par three holes, which get two strokes.

As a business golfer, you will want to establish your handicap and have it revised as your skill level improves. Talk to your club pro about how to do this. It basically involves turning in your signed scorecards for twenty rounds and doing what is necessary to get the paperwork done.

Don't wait until you reach a certain skill level before you have your handicap calculated. Having a handicap helps identify you as a serious business golfer - even if you have a high handicap.

When asked about your handicap, you have three possible answers, depending on your status. If you have had your handicap calculated, give your USGA Handicap Index. This is your basic handicap. You'll be given more strokes on a difficult course and fewer on an easy course, based on the course's slope and course ratings. Don't take these adjustments into consideration when telling someone your handicap - just give your handicap index.

If you haven't had your handicap calculated yet, say so. You can say that you are a beginner and use the beginners maximum of 36 (if that doesn't give you an unfair advantage). Or you may be in the process of having your handicap calculated. Say this, and the others in the foursome will probably help you decide what to use, based on your scores to date. Never respond to a question about your handicap with an estimate of what you *think* it might be. Always be truthful. You either have a handicap, you don't, or you are in the process of getting one. Anything less than total honesty about your handicap can be damaging to your business golf image. That is why it is so important to have your handicap calculated as soon as you decide business golf is for you.

Now suppose that your host knows your handicap and is still interested in getting together. The next step in clarifying the invitation is getting all the details.

When the invitation is first extended, you and your host will probably discuss the course you'll play, the day, and convenient tee times. If you accept, in most cases your host will then set a time to get back to you with further details after the tee time has been reserved. If your host just says, "I'll call you later with the details." and doesn't give a specific day or time for the follow-up call, ask if you can call him or her in a few days to confirm the date. That way if the host doesn't call back, you won't feel awkward calling ""just to check to see if we are still on for next Friday."

When you do confirm the date, get answers to the following questions to make sure you have all the information you need. Rather than trust your memory, be sure to write it down.

Where: Know where you are going and how to get there. This may sound pretty basic, but confirm the name and location of the club. Sometimes golf courses are located near each other and even have similar names. For example, here on Long Island, there are three private clubs within a few miles of each other: Glen Oaks, Glen Head, and Glen Cove. It can get pretty confusing. Ask whatever questions you need to about the general location of the course.

Also get information about the location of the parking lot, the pro shop, and the locker room. Find out where you'll drop off your bag when you get there. Don't forget to find out where you and your host will meet. With all this information, you'll really feel comfortable that you know where you are going.

When: Get both the tee time and the time you'll meet. Make sure that the suggested times give you enough time to warm up and practice. Tell your host if you plan to get there earlier than the suggested time.

If your host wasn't clear about any 19th hole activity such as lunch, dinner, or drinks, you can clarify that at this time by finding out when the round will be over. Add the four to four-and-a-half hours that the round will take to the tee time and say something like, "Then we'll wrap up and be on our way by about six o'clock." Your host should pick up the cue and say something about the 19th hole. If not, you may have a bit of a dilemma.

Because everything at a private club will be on your host's tab, it would be rude of you to suggest lunch or dinner afterward if you are playing at a private club. If you are at a public course, you could suggest a 19th hole activity as your treat. If you are just getting together to play and sharing expenses fifty-fifty, you can inquire if the foursome usually gets together for a drink or lunch after the round. At a private club you could ask the host to be your guest at a restaurant in the vicinity of the club. But then what about the other two people in the foursome?

As you can see, this can be a touchy situation. But the lesson to learn is clear: when you are the host, be very specific about what the invitation includes.

Who: You may already know the others in the foursome. If not, it is appropriate to ask who is rounding out the foursome and to get a little information about them from your host. Naturally, you'll do this without giving your host the third degree. If the foursome was set up to provide a networking opportunity for you, your host will be eager to share this information, and you probably won't even have to ask.

Also find out the name of the head pro so you can introduce yourself when you arrive.

Dress code: This varies from club to club, so ask about the dress code if you are not sure. Ask about the dining room dress code only if dinner is scheduled for the 19th hole. Otherwise your inquiry puts your host in an awkward situation of wondering if you expect dinner, too, and having to say something to clear up the perceived misunderstanding.

If you have any questions later about dress code, location, or any other detail, you can call the club for specific information.

Now that you've clarified the invitation, have all the logistics down pat, and have noted it on your calendar, you'll want to spend some time preparing for the round of business golf.

Prepare

Even if it is just a quick run through of a check list, you'll want to give some thought to what will happen out on the course. You want to make sure you are ready for golf. You also want to make sure you are ready for business.

In business golf, it is critical you know what you are doing on the golf course. So, your preparation for golf involves making sure you are comfortable with everything discussed in earlier chapters. If necessary, polish up in the following areas:

- rules
- etiquette, especially regarding speed of play
- dress and equipment
- technical skill. (I'm not suggesting you try to get your handicap down five strokes before the round. But you may want to go to the driving range or practice green, especially if it has been a while since you've played.)

To prepare for the round of business golf, think about the business agenda and objectives your host might have for the round. What are your expectations? What will be your strategy?

Also think of this in terms of the others in the foursome. Look for opportunities where you could be of benefit to others or you could benefit from others. Always keep your primary business objective of building rapport and developing relationships in mind.

One way of doing this is to give some thought to possible topics of conversation. Chapter 12 covers this in detail because it is an important part of successful business golf. As such, it is important enough to prepare for.

Now you *really* are ready for the round and can hardly wait for the day to arrive. Let's look at the day and see what you can do to earn the reputation of the perfect business golf guest.

Playing the Round

Be sure to give yourself plenty of time so you can get to the club, find your way around, and warm up without feeling rushed. Early afternoon tee times are favored by many business golfers because they can get a half day in at the office. Sometimes, however, it is difficult to get out of the office at a specific time. Always allow yourself enough time. If you arrive at the course feeling rushed, you probably won't play as well. The business relationship could suffer, too, because you won't be as organized and comfortable and it will show.

You'll probably stop at a guard booth on the way to the pro shop, especially if you are playing at a private club. Tell the guard you are a guest and mention your host's name. The guard will probably be expecting you and will often give you information on where to drop off your bag and where to park. If you have any questions and the guard doesn't offer the information, ask. The more information you have, the more you'll know what to expect. You'll feel in control of the situation and be more relaxed. This will be reflected in the image you project.

At a private club there may a valet who will help you with your bag and place it in the bag rack for you. The bag rack is often located just outside the pro shop. For security reasons, at some public courses it may be located just inside the pro shop. Regardless of the type of course, *never* carry your bag into the pro shop. Some public courses will even have posted signs regarding this - for the uninformed who don't realize that carrying a bag into the pro shop is a breach of etiquette.

Your first stop will always be the pro shop, where you'll introduce yourself to the pro, and mention your host's name. The pro should be expecting you and will tell you if your host has arrived yet. If you are at a public course and going fifty-fifty, this is where you'd pay your green fees and cart rental.

While in the pro shop, get a scorecard and study the course layout, yardage, and par information. The serious business golfer knows the importance of course management, so get familiar with the course and start to plan your strategy, at least for the first hole. Also check the scorecard for any special course rules the club may have.

If you are not certain where the locker room is located, ask the pro, because that will be your next stop. At a private club, introduce yourself to the locker room attendant and mention your host's name. You'll be assigned a locker. Go through this process even if all you need to do is change your shoes. Never change your shoes in the parking lot, even if you sometimes see other golfers doing this at a public course. Changing shoes in the parking lot and wearing a hat or visor indoors are two of the most common breaches of business golf etiquette that newcomers are guilty of. The high visibility of these errors is definitely not good for your image. So be aware from head to toe.

Now you are ready to meet your host or await his or her arrival. So you'll head for the pre-arranged meeting place. The locker room attendant will be happy to help you with directions, if necessary.

Although you may have decided to meet at the driving range or practice green instead, the grill is probably the most popular place to get together before the round. Again, introduce yourself and mention your host's name and the waiter will direct you to your host's table.

If your host is already there, great. If not, handle yourself here as you would at a business lunch. Introduce yourself to the other members of the foursome, if they've already arrived. If you arrive first, sit down, relax, and wait. The waiter will ask if you'd like anything. Coffee, tea, or a soft drink are the most appropriate business golf orders. At a private club, this will be put on your host's tab, so there is no need for you to pay. Also, you should not take advantage and order anything more, unless your arrives and suggests lunch.

Once everyone arrives, the conversation will probably switch to golf, if it hasn't already. Handicaps and course conditions will be discussed and side games and wagering will be determined. Chapter 17 focuses in detail on these topics. The important thing to remember is don't be afraid to ask if you don't understand the suggested format or side games. Clarifying everything up front will avoid potential problems later on.

From the grill, you'll usually go to the driving range or practice green to prepare for the round. This will help you relax, get into the mind-set for the round, and limber up the muscles you'll be using. It will also give you some idea of course conditions that day. These are the reasons serious golfers always begin the round with some practice shots. In addition to this, serious business golfers never begin a round without practicing first because of what it communicates about them and the way they do business. Practicing adds to the perception that you are thorough, know the value of preparation, and are willing to take the time necessary to do things right. So even if your warm-up session is brief, always include it as an important part of your pre-round routine.

The order of practice is a personal preference, but for the sake of your body, always begin with some stretching exercises. Beyond that, some golfers prefer to start on the practice green, beginning with short putts to build their confidence. They later move to the driving range and end the session practicing the kind of swing they'll use on the first tee.

Other golfers prefer to loosen up on the driving range and end with the confidence builder of the practice green. Some pragmatic golfers will vary their routine and begin at the practice area that is least crowded, or end at the area closest to the first tee. As a golfer, you will probably develop your own warm-up routine preference. As a business golfer, be aware that your business associates may have different preferences, so be considerate of their choices.

Whatever your warm-up routine, make sure you complete it and are at the first tee with plenty of time to spare before your tee time. Double check that you have everything you need in your pockets - extra balls, tees, ball marker, repair tool. Relax and confidently anticipate a great round of business golf!

The information in the rest of this book, especially Chapters 11 and 12, will help you get through the round successfully. You've prepared and you know what you are doing, so just be a good sport and have fun!

After the 9th hole, you'll probably stop at the refreshment stand or halfway house for something to eat or drink (at a private club, the refreshments will go on your host's tab.) This is also a bathroom break and a chance to use the telephone. If you do want to make a call, ask your host how to use the system to make a credit card call. You don't want your call billed to your host's tab unless you've been given permission to do so.

The 9th hole break is also a great opportunity to discuss the first nine holes and evaluate how the side games are going. By this point, a feeling of camaraderie has often developed because the foursome has faced nine challenging holes together. You may hear some good-natured teasing, and maybe even some not-so-good-natured grumbling. However friendly the foursome is becoming, always remember that it is a round of business golf. The break after the 9th hole often rivals the 19th hole in opportunities to advance the relationship - or damage it. So always be aware of the image you are projecting.

After the 9th hole break, you'll be refreshed and ready to face the challenges of the back nine. New side games, wagering, and presses will probably be discussed sometime during the back nine, if not before. It is also very common that new wagering comes into play just before the 18th hole (everyone's big last chance!) Again, be sure you understand the game that is proposed and if you don't, ask.

Once everyone has putted out on the 18th and scores have been recorded, you'll head back to the pro shop to begin the post-round routine.

Follow Up

Although you may see some recreational golfers at public courses head directly to their car from the 18th green, serious golfers and business golfers know that the round isn't over until all the paperwork is completed.

You will find handicap sheets located near the pro shop (often just outside the door). Your host or whoever is keeping score for the foursome will post your final score for the round. As a guest, your score is recorded on an away sheet that includes the course name and rating, your handicap and score, and your handicap identification number. This is how your handicap is tracked.

Posting scores is important to any serious recreational golfer and to all business golfers. It shows that you follow through, pay attention to details, know the importance of the handicap system, and are conscientious. A discussion of handicaps leads off the round, and posting of scores closes the round. The first and last impression you give as a golfer focuses on handicap. So if you are new to business golf, talk to your pro about getting your handicap calculated. It really is important.

After scores are posted, you'll head back to the locker room to freshen up before the 19th hole. At most private clubs the attendant will take your golf shoes when you enter the locker room. Your shoes will be cleaned while you shower and change clothes.

Common courtesy and good manners apply in the locker room - be neat and place used towels in the designated receptacles. The attendants are there to provide service and offer any assistance they can, not to pick up after you.

When you are ready to leave the locker room, the attendant will return your golf shoes to you. It is appropriate and expected that you tip the attendant for services provided. At a private club, this is the only cash transaction that will take place, other than settling wagers. Everything else is on your host's tab.

While you were using the locker room, your golf bag was probably returned to the bag drop off area. If you have a question about this, ask the attendant, your host, or others in your foursome.

You are now ready for the 19th hole. If you are meeting your host in the dining room, you'll be wearing something that conforms to the dress code.

Because the 19th hole is often the most important hole in business golf, it is discussed in detail in Chapter 18. But whether it is business golf or recreational golf, the 19th hole usually begins with the foursome reuniting to discuss the round and settle up the side games and bets. Always be prepared to *immediately* pay up whatever you owe *in cash*. Win or lose, good sportsmanship is critical at this time.

The others in the foursome may or may not join you and your host for drinks and lunch or dinner. When they announce their departure, extend the usual courtesies and tell them you enjoyed playing with them. If you handled yourself well, someone may suggest getting together again. As a guest, especially at a private club, you probably won't suggest this yourself because it could look like you are fishing for another invitation. But if someone mentions it, you know you've been accepted. This is the perfect opportunity to offer your business card and request theirs, if you haven't done so already.

Somewhere toward the end of the 19th hole, you'll thank your host for the great day you've had and offer to reciprocate. If another date isn't set up, at least arrange for some sort of follow up within the next week. This is not only good manners, it is also good business strategy.

Depending on the relationship you've developed with your host, you'll either send a thank you note the next day, or call to express your appreciation. The thank yous after the 19th hole are expected as a common courtesy. Sending a thank you note really sets you apart as a considerate, appreciative person. It is definitely worth the time and effort.

Since business relationships are based on the principle of reciprocity, thinking about the nature of the relationship and how the round of golf impacted it can help you decide how you will reciprocate. The host may have invited you in order to reciprocate for past business or favors you have done. In that case, the round will bring the relationship back into balance. Your host may expect you'll reciprocate by staying a happy customer and continuing to do business with his company. Depending on the relationship (both business and social), you may decide you also want to reciprocate with lunch, dinner, or a round of golf.

If, on the other hand, your host invited you to provide you with networking opportunities, the reciprocity balance sheet will be out of balance and your obligation to reciprocate will be greater. For example, if the objective was to meet a member of the foursome who represents a large new market for your company and you snag a huge new account as a direct result of the round, you will be eager to show your appreciation to your host.

Chapter 15 looks more closely at the reciprocity issue because it can become an ethical consideration. At this point, be aware that a good business relationship involves a give and take, with both individuals contributing and benefiting from the interactions. Decide how you can reciprocate in a way that will enhance the relationship and keep it in balance.

Very often you will reciprocate in kind - by inviting your host to play a round. You've found a common interest that provides a great opportunity to further develop your business and social relationship, and it is fun! Welcome to the ranks of business golf. Now it is your turn to play host.

When You Are the Host

By this point you should have a great deal of insight into the host's role. As a guest, you've experienced first hand what a good host should be. You know how enjoyable it can be when the host is on top of things - or you know how uncomfortable a guest can feel when the host slips up. This knowledge will serve you well.

Have Experience

If at all possible, do not play host the very first time you ever set foot on a golf course. You want to feel comfortable with the game itself and what happens during a round before you take on the responsibility of entertaining on the golf course.

New business golfers who have the role of host thrust upon them by their companies often find it helpful to delegate or share the responsibility in some way. You can do this by inviting your business associate to an outing where everyone is considered a guest and activities are very structured. You can also enlist the help of a golf buddy who is more familiar with the hosting responsibilities and who would be a welcome addition to the foursome.

Once you feel comfortable playing host, you'll want to do some preliminary planning before you extend the invitation to your business associate.

Do Your Homework

As a guest, you have an idea of all the things that can go wrong or make the day less than perfect. As the host, you'll want to spend time up front making sure that everything is perfect.

Have an objective. Why are you inviting this person to play business golf? Define the purpose of the round. Think about the relationship and what you want to accomplish and also how the round will affect the relationship (the idea of reciprocity, once again). This will help determine the kind of day you'll plan.

Plan the day with your guest in mind. This will really help you develop rapport and build the relationship. It will also help you feel more confident and comfortable, which will definitely affect your business golf image. One of the things to consider is your guest's skill level. A veteran golfer will know the ropes. A new golfer will need more assistance and more information. The guest's skill level will also help you decide on the course to play and whom to include in the foursome.

Obviously, you'll also want a course that offers a challenge equal to your guest's skill level. To determine the degree of difficulty of any course you are considering, check the USGA course and slope ratings for that course. The average course rating in the U.S. is 69.1; the average slope rating is 113. An easy rule of thumb is to compare the course rating to par. When the course rating is higher than par, the course is considered difficult. If in doubt about a certain course, check with the pro.

Beyond that, the course you select will set the tone for the business golf experience and will communicate a message about the value you place on the relationship. So select the course carefully and with your guest in mind. Do you have access to a private club, semi-private club, or resort - or will a public course be appropriate?

Be sensitive to the preferences your guest may have and to the time demands of their business. For example, you probably wouldn't invite an accountant to play during the first two weeks in April (tax time). Many businesses are very busy the beginning or end of the month. Also consider any holidays or religious observances when you select a tentative date for the round.

You also need to consider whom to include in the foursome. Putting together a good foursome is truly an art. You want to assemble a good golf foursome, so you'll consider skill level, personalities, and general interests. You'll also want a good business golf foursome, which might be based on networking opportunities, common business interests, shared markets, or special business expertise. Carefully select your foursome for the benefit it can provide to your guest, both in terms of golf and business.

Some courses will allow twosomes to play at certain times. If this is an option, consider the possible advantages and disadvantages to both you and your guest and decide if a foursome or a twosome is more appropriate.

Finally, choose a 19th hole activity that your guest will enjoy. Make sure it is also compatible with their business schedule and will help you achieve your business golf objective. Some executives prefer breakfast or lunch prior to the round. Some prefer lunch after the 9th hole, and some enjoy drinks and dinner after the round, or a combination of all these activities.

Again, be sensitive to your guest's preferences.

Extend the Invitation

Based on your experience as a guest and the first part of this chapter, you know the ins and outs of extending the invitation, arranging the tee time, and confirming the invitation. Always keep the focus on your guest and pay attention to details, and this will all fall into place.

Before you extend the invitation, think of the most convenient place to meet: the grill, practice green, driving range, or somewhere else. You may even consider car pooling, if it is practical, because it can provide an additional business golf advantage.

Prepare

You'll prepare for both golf and business, just as you did when you were the guest. Because you took the initiative and arranged the golf date, you may have a business objective the guest isn't aware of or doesn't share. Give careful thought to your strategy for meeting your business golf objectives, so you feel comfortable and prepared for the round.

The Day of the Round

Take your cue from your experience as a guest. Think of what your host did well and what could have been done to make it more enjoyable. Use this as a guideline. Then focus on your guest and do everything you can to ensure an enjoyable day. This may mean playing customer golf or changing your business agenda, if necessary. The important thing is to make sure your guest has a good time. That will almost guaranteed a successful round of business golf.

Summary

Business golf often begins with someone extending an invitation to join a foursome for a round of golf. Whether you are the guest or the host, your knowledge of business golf etiquette will allow you to feel comfortable and confident during the round and will determine how successful you will be at using golf as a business tool.

The Back Nine of Business Golf
Using Golf Outings Effectively

Andrew Carnegie presented Yale University with $200,000 to build a golf course because he believed, "Golf is an indispensable adjunct to high civilization." No doubt Carnegie would agree that golf is also an indispensable adjunct to business. U.S. Steel was born out of a deal that was conceived on the Golf course.

Carnegie may or may not have been the first person to combine golf with business, but he definitely wasn't the last! As golf grew in popularity, more and more golfers recognized the value of golf as a business tool. It didn't take business long to decide to leverage the opportunities that exist in business golf. If playing in foursomes was good business, playing with larger groups had to be even better business! Instead of a foursome, why not an outing? Especially when outings offer so many additional advantages.

Advantages of Outings

Playing in foursomes will probably never be replaced as the basic format for business golf. But because outings greatly expand business opportunities and are available in so many different formats, both large and small businesses are using them more and more.

Flexibility

Golf outings can be defined as organized events that include more than four people and more than just a round of golf. They can be sponsored by charities, civic or social organizations, or businesses, and can be planned and coordinated by the sponsoring group or by professional planners. Many golf outings are one-day local events, but three- day formats at resorts, and even one-or-two week vacations to foreign countries are increasing in popularity. Obviously, the more elaborate the format, the more expensive the event. Although in the strictest sense "outings" include actually playing golf, many businesses have broadened the definition and now also use spectator golf (attending a competitive event strictly as an observer) as the basis of an outing.

This flexibility in the format of an outing gives business a wide range of opportunities. Whatever the business golf objective, there is certain to be a type of outing that is appropriate and that can be tailored to specific needs.

Outings are Time and Cost-Effective

Whether you attend a charity outing alone as a networking opportunity or your company sponsors an outing and invites 100 clients and suppliers, outings maximize the number of business associates you can reach within a given time frame and budget. Depending on how the outing is structured and who is participating, a synergy often develops that results in more business opportunities than if each participant simply interacted with every other participant on a one-to-one basis.

Outings Often Allow You to Control More Variables

Corporate outings are specifically designed to meet the needs of the sponsoring organization. One-day outings are often held on days when the course is closed to other golfers. This gives the outing planners greater control. They can select the format of play that best suits their purpose without worrying about slowing play for other golfers. Special menus can be selected, and meetings and other activities such as skill clinics can be scheduled without disrupting the club's usual routine. The sponsoring organization has greater control over the total environment because everyone attending the outing is an invited guest.

Although you don't have this much control when you use outings sponsored by charities and civic organizations, you can determine the overall environment based on the outing you select. Different outings project different images, based on the sponsoring organization, the course played, and the people the outing usually attracts. The outing is a self-contained unit, which the business golfer selects. This allows for more control than when playing in a foursome where the environment is more fluid. Charity and civic outings also give the business golfer more control of time, because many of the planning details associated with playing in a foursome are handled by the sponsoring organization.

Outings Are Events

Because outings are more elaborate than a simple round of golf, they are often perceived as events, especially when celebrities are playing. Depending on the outing, there may be an air of excitement and a sense of status and prestige associated with it. Part of this is related to the specifics of the event (the course, gifts, celebrities), and part is due to the group dynamics that occur during the event. These positive feelings make it much easier to develop rapport and build relationships and also cause outings to carry greater weight in the reciprocity equation.

Non-golfers Can Participate

Outings can be a great non-threatening introduction to business golf because they often use a format that allows low skill and non -golfers to play and enjoy the game. Many business golfers have found that clients who seldom golf and may not be interested in playing in a foursome are often very interested in outings.

Whether you are a veteran golfer or a non-golfer, there are several things to keep in mind when you're the guest.

When You Are the Guest

If you've read this far, you know about dress, equipment, the importance of etiquette, and how to behave when you are invited to play in a foursome. Even if you've never played before, you are off to a good start, because you'll use the same information and skills when you play in an outing. You'll also need additional information.

At an Outing

When you are invited to an outing that is a corporate event, it is pretty safe to assume that you are a guest. Although sometimes the invitation will be verbal, it is more common that you'll receive a written invitation that will include all the details. Good business etiquette requires you to respond as soon as possible.

You may be extended an invitation by a business associate to attend a charity or civic outing. This will usually be a verbal invitation and may need to be clarified. The associate may be trying to get a foursome together or may be working on behalf of the charity and "selling foursomes." Or you may be invited as a guest. Be very clear what the arrangements are.

At most outings there is usually a central meeting area and registration table where everyone signs in, receives a gift bag and rules for the day, as well as information on the outing setup. You may be directed to another area for activities such as putting contests, skills clinics, or pre-round brunch or lunch.

If it is a charity or civic outing, the person at the registration table may also ask you to purchase raffle tickets or participate in some other game of chance. At some outings the raffle tickets are sold after the round during drinks or dinner. Whether you are a guest or attending on your own, good business etiquette requires you to participate. The outing is after all, a fund-raiser, so you'll want to support the sponsoring organization in this way.

After the round, instead of posting your scores, you'll turn in your scorecard. The pro or the outing planner will handle the calculations to determine the winners of the various events.

The 19th hole activities will vary depending on the outing, but will often include an open bar followed by dinner. Winners for the round are usually announced and raffles are drawn after dinner. There may also be a speech, especially if the event includes a celebrity golfer.

Conduct yourself during these activities as you would at a business dinner party. Consider why your host invited you, your own business golf agenda, and the structure of the event to determine how much mixing and mingling with other guests is appropriate. For example, at a corporate gathering with assigned seating, your host may formally introduce you and your interactions may be pretty much limited to those at your table. With an open bar and buffet dinner arrangement, informal self introductions and greater networking activity may be the order of the day. Play it by ear, and, as always, remember it is business golf and don't do anything to damage your relationship with your host.

The day after the outing you'll want to send a written thank you to your host. Be sure the note is personalized and includes references to specific events (a particularly challenging hole, a well-hit shot, a gift you received). Tastes vary, but many business people believe a handwritten note works best. It is more personal and can be perceived as warmer and more sincere than a letter typed by your secretary. Of course the best way to really show your appreciation is to reciprocate appropriately. Decide how to reciprocate just as you would if you had been the guest in a foursome.

At a Spectator Event

Based on your relationship with the corporate sponsor, your invitation to a professional tour event could include admission passes, tickets to the hospitality tent, or even an invitation to play in the pro-am event. You may or may not even see your host, depending on whether the tickets were given as a gift or an invitation was extended to get together.

If you are lucky enough to rate a slot in the pro-am event, you are probably a veteran golfer who has played in many outings and attended many spectator events. By the time you play in the pro-am event, your golf etiquette and business golf savvy are probably beyond reproach. But if you are not a golfer or have never attended a spectator event, you'll want to be acquainted with the do's and don'ts of tour events.

Although you can enjoy the event without knowing about golf etiquette and rules, it probably would help to at least watch a golf event on TV to get a feel for it. Attending a tour event is different than attending a baseball game or hockey match and you'll want to make sure that your behavior is appropriate.

There is no dress code for spectators at most tournaments, but since the majority of people attending are golfers, standard golf attire is the popular choice - without the spikes, of course. You may see some blue jeans and tee shirts, but that is not the norm and not a good business golf choice. Wear comfortable shoes because you'll probably do a lot of walking. Don't forget a visor or hat and sunscreen. Shady spots are often few and far between.

At the entrance to the tournament you'll probably receive a program with a map of the course that includes the locations of rest rooms, hospitality tents and grandstands, par and yardage information, tee times and pairings for the day, scores from previous days, and other spectator information (as well as a lot of ads for corporate sponsors). Read the program carefully and decide your plan of action for the day, if your host hasn't already done so.

Tips for spectators may also be included in the program.

"Contained enthusiasm" is an apt description of the general atmosphere and appropriate behavior style. Comedian David Brenner, who said he doesn't watch golf on TV because he can't stand whispering, was exaggerating a bit about the hushed, sedate nature of spectator golf. While you won't always whisper, you will always want to keep in mind the genteel nature of the game and how your behavior can directly impact the players' ability to concentrate.

Follow the same golf etiquette you would when you are in a foursome and another player is preparing to swing. Be quiet and still, especially when a marshall says "quiet" or "stand." Don't make any movements or noises that could distract a player.

Applause is appropriate after a well-hit shot, but there is no "rooting for the home team" or player. Recognize and appreciate all demonstrations of skill with your applause. Never cheer anyone's misfortune. Of course, hooting, hollering, and booing are definitely inappropriate.

Cameras, coolers, and radios are usually not allowed. Cameras are sometimes allowed during the practice rounds or pro-am, but they create a distraction for the players and are prohibited during the actual tournament. Coolers and radios are almost always banned. Even if they aren't, they are not part of the image you want to project.

Autographs are signed after the round. There is often an area outside the scoring tent where fans congregate to meet the pros and get autographs. Never approach a player for an autograph during the round. Also, don't distract a player by asking for an autograph after the 18th hole. The round isn't over until the paperwork is done. You wouldn't want to be responsible for anyone making a Roberto deVicenzo- type error in scoring.

Have respect for the players' time and don't ask for an autograph unless it is important to you. If you are a golf fan, great, - get the autograph. Or if you have a business associate who would appreciate it, you can really parlay your business golf opportunities by getting the autograph. But don't waste the pro's time if you really don't want the autograph. Lee Trevino, for example, tells about signing a five dollar bill for a fan who said she was so thrilled that she'd keep it all her life. Later when Trevino bought drinks, the autographed bill was in with the change he received! Appreciate the value of the autographs you get, or don't waste everyone's time getting them.

Have a strategy to get the most out of the event. A golf course is large and you won't be able to see everything. Decide how you can maximize your enjoyment (and possible business opportunities) throughout the day.

Some spectators enjoy following a certain player throughout the round. Others select a particular hole and enjoy watching all the players meet the challenges of that hole. The first tee is a popular location early in the day. Later the center of activity is the 18th green. Bleachers are often located at the more popular locations. Decide what your basic game plan will be for the day.

If you are on your own and not spending time with your host, your business golf opportunities will be rather limited. You may strike up conversations with other spectators, especially if you are following one player or staying at one hole during the entire round. You also may see business associates that you normally don't have easy access to but can approach more easily in this relaxed, social setting. But basically, your agenda will be fun, not business.

The spectator event can, however, create business golf opportunities for you in the future. Be very observant and look for things that will make good business golf conversation somewhere down the line. Make mental notes on how the pros handle certain challenges and how they interact with the crowd. Talk to the volunteers and marshals. You may hear some great inside stories that could help you develop rapport with some business associate, even years from now.

Make a conscious effort to use the experience to enrich your background as a business golfer. And use one bit of information or story you hear to personalize the thank you note you send to your host the next day!

When You Are the Host

After you attend a few outings and discover the many business opportunities they offer, it probably won't be long before you decide to play host. You'll want to choose the type of event carefully so that you get the most benefit for your money and everyone has a good time.

At a Charity or Civic Outing

These events are a wonderful opportunity to entertain clients or employees without having to do all the planning and organizing yourself. You'll still have the basic hosting responsibilities mentioned in the section on hosting a foursome, but you'll "delegate" some of the work and won't have to worry about as many details. But because the event becomes a reflection of you, you'll want to choose the outing carefully.

Know the event. If you haven't attended it before, talk to someone who did. Select an outing based on what your guest would enjoy, just as you select the course and 19th hole activity to suit your guest when you play in a foursome. Make sure that the outing has the quality image you want to project.

Plan the foursome carefully before you extend the invitation. A popular pairing includes two players from the host company and two invited guests. As with any business golf foursome you arrange, think of combining people who will enjoy golf and conversation with each other and who can also provide business opportunities for each other.

If you know other business golfers who are attending, you can also provide your guests with a broader networking opportunity. Some companies ensure bringing together the right blend of people by sponsoring their own outing. Although it is more work, it also provides you with more control over the many details involved and can result in greater business benefits.

Sponsoring Your Own Outing

You and your company may find you are using business golf so much that you decide having your own outing would be more efficient. You could entertain more clients or employees at one time and could design an agenda to meet your specific objectives.

Ask any company that sponsors its own outing and they'll probably tell you it is great for business and worth every penny spent. They'll probably also tell you that it is expensive and involves a lot of work. So know what you are doing and what you are getting yourself into, because if the outing is not done well, it can really hurt you.

Make the decision to sponsor an outing only after you look at all the variables involved. Too often companies make an emotional decision because golf is fun and having an outing is prestigious. If they use business golf a lot, it is easy to just say, "Let's do it.", because it looks like a good decision. Ask yourself these questions to make sure an outing is right for you and your company.

Why do you want to have an outing? What is your business objective? What results do you want to achieve? Is having an outing the most efficient way to do this, in terms of time and money?

For example, your objective may be employee team building. You may expect the outing to result in improved communication between employees and departments, which might be measured by an increase in productivity, a decrease in errors, faster turn around time, or fewer complaints. You may decide an outing is the best way to do this because it can be designed to let the team get to know each other in a social setting and can also include a more formal team-building program. You believe nothing else can do this for you as efficiently.

On the other hand, maybe your objective is to thank clients for past business. As a result of the outing, you hope the clients will continue to do business with you. Perhaps you could achieve the same results spending less time and money if you invited them to a spectator event instead.

As you think about why you want to have an outing, you'll automatically think about the next variable.

Who will attend? Do you want to invite clients, employees, prospects, suppliers, or various people from all these categories? What criteria will you use to determine who is invited? Will it be clients who give you more than, say, $10,000 worth of business a year or employees whose performance is at or above a certain standard? Also think of who should be invited in terms of the criteria for putting together any good foursome: who'll have fun playing golf and interacting together and also provide business and networking opportunities for each other.

Give the selection criteria and possible guest list serious thought. The success of the outing in large part depends on it. You can do harm to your image and lose business by inviting the wrong blend of people. You can also create hard feelings and damage relationships if you don't invite some people who find out about the event and feel they should have been invited.

Looking at a possible guest list can also help you decide whether you really want to have an outing. If the guest list snowballs, you may want to consider alternatives - a hospitality tent at a spectator event, for example. Or you may want to redefine your selection criteria and plan several events with different groups. The selection criteria will also help you decide the type of event to have.

What type of event and can you afford it? The type of event you choose will be based on two things: your guest list (the more important the people are to you, the more elaborate the event you'll plan) and your budget. Once you've decided to have the outing, you'll focus in on all the details of the event. For now, think in broader terms to help decide what type of outing to have *if* you do have one and how it fits in your budget. Things to consider include:

- What is the length of the event? Is a one-day local outing or a three-day trip more appropriate? You may want to consider something even more elaborate (a trip to the Masters Tournament?) for some of your more valuable clients or employees.
- Will business meetings as well as golf be on the agenda? If so, you'll need a facility that can accommodate this. Weigh the additional expense against the results you expect.
- Will spouses also be invited? Although significant others are more often included in longer events, some companies do invite them to participate in one-day outings as well.
- Where would the event take place? Think of upscale, top -quality locations that fit within your budget and can accommodate the event you have in mind. If you can't afford something top notch, look at your objective again and plan an event on a smaller scale so you won't have to sacrifice quality.
- Will you use celebrity golfers? You'll find a lot more senior-level executives interested in attending your outing if celebrity golfers are part of it.

When you use this process to decide whether or not to sponsor an outing, you begin to realize how complicated planning an event really is. This leads you to the final question to consider before you make the decision to have your own event.

Who will organize and coordinate the outing? This decision is very important, so give it a lot of thought because the success of the outing depends on it. Your guests will tend to remember the one thing that goes wrong at the outing rather than all the things that go well. Make sure the person responsible for planning the event has the time and expertise to do a good job.

The easiest way to guarantee that the event will be a success is to delegate the responsibility to a company that specializes in planning corporate golf outings. Some meeting planners and travel agents also offer this service. These professionals can tailor an event to meet your needs and fit your budget. They also work with many facilities, courses, and golf pros that your in-house staff may not have access to. Many companies have found it very cost- effective to use these professional planners.

Some large corporations have their own meeting planner on staff who is experienced and has the contacts to organize a successful outing. Other companies underestimate the amount of work involved and delegate the planning to someone in human resources, sales, or marketing who is already overworked.

If you are planning the event yourself, be sure to enlist the help of the golf pro at the course you select. Some clubs and most resorts also have a corporate events planner who can be a big help in handling some of the details for you.

If you are new to outing planning, check the Resource Section of this book for publications that provide information on putting together an outing, tournament or competition. John Marshall's *Corporate Golf Outing Management* is especially helpful. It is a procedures manual that details everything you need to know to run an outing. Marshall has served as a tournament consultant on PGA Tour events and is an authority on organizing and managing corporate golf outings. His book goes into all the planning details that are beyond the scope of this book. However, Marshall and several other planning pros did share some secrets to success in sponsoring an outing.

Tips From Outing Planning Pros

Always pay attention to quality.   Everything about the outing is a reflection of you and your business. Don't skimp. If your budget is limited, plan a smaller event rather than cutting corners. A top-quality brunch or lunch, for example, does more for your image and business than a mediocre dinner.

Select the course carefully.   An exclusive club or championship course people don't get to play often contributes to your quality image. It will also often attract the head honchos and decision makers who might decline a less appealing invitation.

Pay special attention to pairings. Plan everything with your guests' interests and needs in mind.

Get expert help. Even if you don't use a professional planner, do use the services of the club pro and anyone else available through the club or resort. This will help guarantee a successful outing. These professionals will also have a greater sense of accountability, since customer service is part of their job description and they want to keep you as a client.

Select gifts and prizes that are special and will continue to promote you to your guests.

- Choose nontraditional items, since most golfers have a good supply of golf related products.
- Include your company name and the date and location of the event on the gift, if possible.
- Select something your guests will use frequently over a long period of time.
- Choose quality items that convey to your guests you think they are special, but avoid anything that conveys extravagance. The gifts you give at this outing set the expectations for the next outing. Avoid getting into the "can you top this" trap.
- Team photos make great souvenirs, especially if celebrity players are included. Mounting or framing the photos and delivering them the following week is a great way to follow up with your guests.

Do an in-person site inspection. Regardless of the reputation of the facility, examine the course, locker rooms, dining area, pro shop, and, if appropriate, meeting rooms and hotel accommodations. Make sure everything is top notch and will meet the needs of your guests.

Select celebrity players based on personality, as well as name value or status. You may gain more business benefit using two or three good, well-known players than one superstar.

Enjoy the event yourself. Plan ahead and get whatever help you need to make sure everything goes well. But during the event, keep your focus on your guests. They'll enjoy it more if you are an active participant - and it will do more to develop your relationship with them, too. Delegate the last-minute, behind-the-scenes tasks so you can relax, have fun, and focus on your primary objective - keeping your guests happy.

Summary

Outings can be the most efficient and cost-effective form of business golf because they maximize your business opportunities. The secret lies in bringing together the right blend of people and making sure the outing projects a quality image for you and your company.

Events sponsored by civic and charitable organizations are great for networking. They are also a convenient way to entertain clients or prospects without doing all the work yourself. The key to success is choosing the outing carefully.

Many companies decide to run their own event because it gives them greater control and flexibility. Organizing and planning an event involves a lot of details and a lot of time. Your image can be easily damaged if things go wrong or the outing isn't perceived as a quality event. To maximize your chances of success, make your decision to run an event only after considering all the variables involved. Also get professionals to help you, whether it is the golf pro and the club events planner or a company that specializes in corporate outings.

Whether you decide to use an outing or to play in a foursome, you'll want to make sure you are comfortable with the conversation during the round. Will it include business? When should business be discussed? How will all the members of the foursome get along?

Before you plan this part of your business golf strategy, you have to know how to read people. That begins with the inner foursome of personal behavioral styles, discussed in the next chapter.

The Inner Foursome
Golf Behavioral Styles

The number "four" seems to have a special significance in golf. The game is usually played in a foursome. A well-paced round takes about four hours to play. And you yell, "Fore!" when you believe someone may be hit by your ball.

In professional golf, four events make up "The Majors" - The Masters, the U.S. Open, the British Open, and the PGA Championship. And only four men have won all four Majors: Gene Sarazen, Ben Hogan, Jack Nicklaus, and Gary Player.

Four also has some significance in explaining human behavior. Throughout history, many personality and behavior theories have been based on models that identify four basic styles. For example, astrology, which was considered a science in ancient times, assigns the twelve signs of the Zodiac into four basic types: Earth, Air, Fire, and Water. Hippocrates defined personality and behavior using a model based on four temperaments: choleric, melancholic, sanguine, and phlegmatic.

In more modern times, Alfred Adler applied the four temperaments to his activity-social interest model and came up with four personality types: the ruling type (choleric), the avoiding type (melancholic), the socially useful type (sanguine), and the getting type (phlegmatic). Carl Jung, meanwhile, defined four psychological types (intuitor, thinker, feeler, sensor) in terms of the ego attitudes of extroversion and introversion.

It didn't take business long to adapt some of these models to help explain behavior styles in the work place and to improve employee

117

effectiveness. The Myers-Briggs Type Indicator, based on Jung's model, is widely used in business. It applies two tendencies (Jung's ego attitudes) to four behavior categories (Jung's psychological types) and looks at an individual's personality in terms of four index preferences.

The Social Styles model, based on the work of David Merrill, Ph.D., focuses on assertiveness and responsiveness as well as task and relationship orientation to determine whether your basic behavioral style is Driving, Expressive, Amiable, or Analytical.

The Dimensions of Behavior model, based on the work of William Moulton Marston and John Geier, Ph.D., looks at whether you perceive your environment as favorable or antagonistic and how much power you feel you have over it. The combination of these four dimensions determines your behavioral style.

The Situational Leadership, which was developed by Paul Hersey and Ken Blanchard, focuses on four leadership styles: Delegating, Participating, Selling, and Telling.

Maybe sometime during your career you've taken an inventory or survey based on one of these models and you know your basic personality or behavioral style. Knowing a model can also help you to recognize the personality or behavioral patterns of others and, hopefully, to work more effectively with them.

What does all this have to do with business golf? Everything! As I have said repeatedly, your primary objective in business golf is always developing rapport and building the relationship. Knowing your own style and knowing how to read someone else's style is a critical skill necessary to reaching that objective. Without a model to help you read people, you'll gain your people savvy through trial and error - and probably have some rocky relationships along the way and may even lose some business. A good model to start with is the Golf Archetypes Model described in the Hyatt Study.

Golf Archetypes - The Hyatt Model

The Hyatt Study found four basic profiles or "archetypes" among the executive golfers surveyed. Each group has a distinct way of handling themselves in both golf and business.

1. **Gunslingers** are gamblers and risk-takers. They look for any edge they can get and are more likely to cheat. They play more frequently than the other groups and are into high tech, special equipment. Gunslingers made up 12 percent of the sample; 87 percent were males.
2. **Non-Competitors** think golf is fun, but just a game. They aren't risk-takers. They play to relax, prefer less challenging courses, and don't let the game get to them. They also have higher handicaps. This

was the second largest group in the study (32 percent of the executives). The majority (57 percent) of the women were in this group.

3. **Escapists** are competitive golfers who always play to win and
   often lose their temper during a round. They've been playing
   longer than the executives in the other groups and their vacations
   usually include golf. Escapists accounted for 12 percent of the
   sample. Only 11 percent of the women fell into this category.

4. **Power Players** strongly associate golf with business and want to
   be challenged by both. They are the most fanatical golfers and
   have the lowest handicaps. They are very competitive, prefer difficult courses, lose their temper when playing badly, play in bad
   weather, and spend the most on equipment. The largest percent
   age (44 percent) of executives surveyed were in this category.
   Almost half (49 percent) of the males were Power Players. The
   women golfers with the lowest handicaps and the highest incomes
   were in this group.

A basic understanding of the archetypes will help you determine
someone's attitude toward golf, or just how serious they are about the
game. This will help you adapt your business golf strategy. For example,
a Power Player would probably expect to talk business during the round.
An Escapist would probably be annoyed if you did.

Matching your style to the archetype profile of the person you are
playing with will help you develop the relationship much more quickly,
even if you don't talk business during the round.

The Behavioral Types Model

Using a second model will provide you with even more information
about your business golf associates. It will help you not only look at how
people relate to golf or business, but also how they relate to each other.

This model focuses on behavior, which is external and observable,
rather than on personality, which is internal and unobservable as well as
more complex and harder to change. The model is presented in detail in
*People Smarts: Bending the Golden Rule to Give Others What They
Want*, an excellent, easy-to-read book by Tony Alessandra and Michael
O'Connor. You'll want to read it to get a thorough understanding of the
four behavioral styles, which they call the Director, the Socializer, the
Relater, and the Thinker.

The four behavioral styles are based on an individual's level of
directness and openness. Behavior clues can also be looked at in terms of
how a person relates to tasks and relationships as well as their pace in
doing so.

Although most people are a blend of the four styles, they usually have a high *natural* tendency toward one of the styles, with an almost as high *acquired* tendency toward a secondary style. When you understand these styles, know your own style, and can read another person's, you can make behavior choices that will enhance your relationships because you will treat others the way they want to be treated. This will not only help you in business and business golf, but in every area of your life as well.

Let's look briefly at some of the behavioral characteristics of the four basic styles. As you read about each one, you'll probably think of people you know who behave in a similar way.

The Director

Directors focus more on the task than on relationships. They are fast-paced and more concerned with the bottom line than with details. They are most comfortable when they are in control of the situation. Therefore, they enjoy being in positions of power and authority and try hard to be the best and win.

These individuals are self-confident, make decisions easily, and are risk-takers. They are interested in action and become impatient with small talk and hesitancy over details.

People with this style are very direct and may seem to lack concern for others because of their abruptness and their focus on results.

The Director is the behavioral style that comes to mind when you think of a typical CEO.

The Socializer

The name Socializer tells you these individuals are people- and relationship-oriented rather than task-oriented. Like the Director, they also enjoy controlling the situation, but do so through people. They motivate, persuade, entertain, and like to make a favorable impression on others.

Socializers tend to be fast-paced. They enjoy groups of people and group activities and have a strong need for recognition. They like being in the spotlight and are often trendsetters who enjoy being the first with the latest style.

People with this behavioral tendency are usually optimistic. They can often be over-optimistic, especially about their own abilities. Because they are not task-oriented, they don't enjoy details, can be disorganized, and may not follow through. They value freedom of expression and dislike structure or anything that controls their freedom.

Socializers are often found in the sales and marketing departments within an organization.

The Relater

Relaters are very reliable and predictable. They prefer a secure, steady environment and are not risk-takers. They enjoy tradition, like to maintain the status quo, and tend to resist change. This can cause them to be stubborn at times.

This behavioral style is characterized by a steady approach to tasks. Relaters often stay with one job or company for a long period to time. They are loyal, will concentrate on getting the task done, and prefer to follow established work routines. Relaters are usually conservative in their dress and life-style choices.

Although they are concerned with tasks, Relaters are people- and relationship-oriented. They prefer to cooperate with others in getting the job done and are great team players. They have patience, are good listeners, and have an easygoing, slower-paced approach to people. They are not as outgoing as the Socializer, but they enjoy close relationships and are often very family-oriented. They may prefer a job that doesn't infringe on their personal life.

Relaters often fill administrative functions within a company. Also, because of their concern for both tasks and people, Relaters do well in customer service or sales roles.

The Thinker

Like the Director, the Thinker is also more task- than people- and relationship-oriented. Thinkers, however, are slower paced and much more concerned with details. They prefer to follow procedures, focus on quality, and check for details. They are very factual and analytical and have a tendency to be perfectionists. This can make them very critical of themselves and very demanding of others.

Although Thinkers are diplomatic with people, they prefer small groups and people they know and are often quiet, cool, and distant. They are very observant of what is happening around them, but tend to hold in their feelings. Their conversations are usually brief and to the point.

Thinkers are usually very meticulous about their grooming and personal possessions. Their choices are usually conservative, with a focus on quality and efficiency.

In the corporate setting, auditors and accountants are often Thinkers.

As you read through the styles, you may have recognized people you know, although not all the characteristics mentioned may have been on target. That is because we're all a blend of the styles and possess these characteristic behaviors to various degrees. We've also learned to modify our styles. We choose behaviors most appropriate to the particular role we are in. So although someone is a Socializer, for example, at work she may be organized and detail-oriented because she has adapted her behavioral tendencies to the requirements of her job.

Even though the styles aren't always 100 percent on target, the styles do give us a model for making some sense of what people's words and actions are telling us.

A Closer Look at the Four Styles

With this in mind, let's look at several golf pros. See if you can identify a *possible* behavioral style based on some specific behavior examples and what others observe about them.

Arnold Palmer

In his book *They Call Me Super Mex*, Lee Trevino described Arnold Palmer in this way: "He was aggressive. He might be leading by one or two shots, but he wouldn't be cautious. He'd go for the flag from the middle of an alligator's back."

At the 1968 U.S. Open, Arnold Palmer said, "My putting was atrocious. I changed grips, stance, you name it. I tried everything but standing on my head."

Nathaniel (Ironman) Avery had this to say about him at the 1962 Masters: "When Mr. Palmer's getting ready to make his move, he jerks at that glove, pulls up his britches, and starts walking fast. When he does that, everybody better watch out. He's gonna stampede anything that gets in his way."

In 1984 at the U.S. Senior Open, Arnold Palmer said, "If you are stupid enough to whiff, you should be smart enough to forget it."

If you spotted these as examples of Director behavior, you are right. Fast-paced, results-oriented, direct, and to the point. But what about Arnold Palmer's legendary people skills? Think about Arnie's Army (his devoted fans following during a round) and his charismatic appeal and you might identify him as a Socializer. His secondary tendencies do fall into that style, but he's more strongly task-oriented. This combination of high Director behavior with strong Socializer tendencies is typical of people with great charisma (John F. Kennedy is another example).

Fuzzy Zoeller

Fuzzy has said, "I didn't need to finish college to know what golf was all about. All you need to know is to hit the ball, find it, and hit it again until it disappears into the hole in the ground."

At the 1984 PGA Championship, he said, "The way I hit the ball today, I need to go to the range. Instead, I think I'll go to the bar."

Dan Jenkins in *Sports Illustrated* described Fuzzy this way: "Hit it, go find it, hit it again. Grin, have a smoke, take a sip, make a joke and every so often win a major championship."

From these comments, it is apparent that Fuzzy Zoeller is not strongly task-oriented. He is focused more on the process (hit it, find it, hit it again) than on the results (winning), so he doesn't fit the Director style. He also doesn't sound like a cautious, detail-oriented, self-critical perfectionist (the Thinker).

You may not be able to tell from this limited information whether Fuzzy is a Socializer or a Relater. I would guess he is a Socializer with secondary tendencies of the Relater style. He sounds like the life-of-the-party type who is outgoing and enjoys the spotlight. This is also confirmed by what I've observed watching the pro tour on TV: Fuzzy waving a white flag in mock surrender, his interaction with the fans, and his reputation for partying.

His easy-going manner and relaxed pace are characteristics of a Relater. Dan Jenkins' comment about Fuzzy winning a major champion-ship every so often is also consistent with this style, which is known for its steady approach to getting tasks done. The Socializer style with high Relater tendencies is the style of someone who enjoys the game for its own sake, which certainly sounds like Fuzzy Zoeller.

Seve Ballesteros

Golf Magazine asked Seve Ballesteros the difference between playing on the pro tour and playing anywhere else. Seve said: "More money. Otherwise, no difference. Birdie the same. Par the same. Bogey the same. Out-of-bounds the same."

Ben Crenshaw has said, "Seve's never in trouble. We see him in the trees quite a lot, but that looks normal to him."

When he was growing up in Spain, Seve only had a 3-iron. He practiced and practiced, using that one club. He said, "You learn to do everything with that club. It makes you think things up that you never would if you had all the clubs."

Seve's also said that during major tournaments he "lives in a bubble." People are talking, but he is concentrating so hard he just doesn't hear them.

All this sounds like a Relater pattern. The steady, determined approach to the task of mastering that 3-iron. The ability to concentrate on a task, although the normal tendency is to be people-oriented (if he was totally task-oriented, he wouldn't have to put up the bubble to isolate himself). He saw the pro tour as basically the same as playing elsewhere. This is consistent with a Relater's preference for a steady environment and desire to maintain the status quo. Ben Crenshaw's comment describes reliable, predictable behavior and a person with a great deal of patience who takes things in stride. These are all characteristics of the Relater pattern.

Ben Crenshaw

In 1983 at the Sea Pines Heritage Classic, Ben Crenshaw hit three balls into the water to score an eleven on the 14th hole. He later said, "I was stubborn. I knew the 4-iron was the right club."

He has described golf this way: "This is the hardest game in the world. There is no way a golfer can think he is really something, because that's when the game gets you." He has also said his philosophy is, "Never do anything stupid."

During the late seventies, Crenshaw said, "I've got to blow dry my hair or I've got to withdraw from the tournament. I don't play anywhere unless I can blow dry my hair."

When Crenshaw was nine years old, he took his first lesson with Harvey Penick, who told Ben to hit the ball. He did, and put it on the green. Harvey Penick was pleased and asked Ben to put it in the hole. Crenshaw replied, "Why didn't you tell me that in the first place." Then he teed up another ball and hit a hole-in-one.

These quotes and stories probably brought to mind the Thinker pattern. Someone who is realistic and logical and uses caution rather than taking risks (consider his philosophy). Someone who likes to be right and can be self-critical (the 4-iron *was* the right club). A meticulously groomed individual who is concerned with details. And someone who likes to know the why and the how, and asks brief, to the point questions.

Looking at the specific behavior of individuals as you did in this exercise and relating it to the four styles can give you some insight into why others behave as they do and the reason they react to your behavior in certain ways. It also tells you something about how individuals prefer to be treated, so you can adapt your behavior accordingly.

But before you look at specific behaviors for clues to someone's style, it is important to have the right perspective about the styles and how you adapt to them. Because despite first impressions, Arnold Palmer may not be a Director after all.

Things to Keep in Mind About Behavioral Styles

You can't pigeonhole people. Human behavior is very complex. It is unrealistic and impossible to expect to categorize all people into a few simple patterns. But if you've known someone long enough, like a family member or friend, you probably have some ideas about what they'll do and how they'll behave in certain situations. Your observations over time let you know what kind of person they are.

The behavior model simply helps you do the same thing, only more efficiently. If we start with behavioral tendencies that are true for the general population in most cases and we're more consciously observant, we can get to "know" people a lot faster and even get along with them better. But remember, we're always dealing with behavioral *tendencies*, so the model can't be 100 percent on target.

Everyone is a blend of the different styles. Most people have a primary natural style and a secondary acquired style, which is based on their experiences. And although we have a tendency toward a particular style and feel most comfortable with that style, we all have a "behavior repertoire" that is made up of all the styles. (Alessandra and O'Connor have identified sixteen common patterns of mixed styles.)

There's no right or wrong style. Any style can be successful in any occupation or pursuit. Some may seem like a more natural fit. But anyone can build on any of their behavioral tendencies and become successful by meeting the requirements of the role. For example, all four styles are represented on the pro tour. A Socializer, however, may have to focus more on his task-related behaviors to keep his skills sharp. This may not be a natural behavioral tendency, but it can certainly be a behavior choice. A Thinker would probably choose to work on his people skills if he wanted to become a successful and in-demand celebrity golfer.

Some behavioral patterns are pretty consistent throughout life (natural tendencies) but can be changed or modified (acquired tendencies), especially as a result of major life events. I used an example of Ben Crenshaw's behavior at age nine to make a point. In fact, a lot could have happened in his life since then. He could be a completely different person. Or he could be the same. Which brings us to our next point.

It is hard to determine a behavioral style on the basis of limited information. Jumping to conclusions about behavioral styles is as risky as jumping to conclusions about anything else. The more behavior you observe and the more information you collect over a period of time, the better you'll know a person.

We adapt our styles and behavior to meet the expectations of other people and society. All of us have learned that certain behaviors are appropriate in certain situations. For example, our primary tendency may not be the style of a Thinker or Relater. But many of us have adapted our style toward those patterns to meet the requirements of school and work:

we follow a set routine, we conform to rules, regulations and procedures, and we may become more detail-oriented. Adapting is part of the socialization process and serves us well by helping us stay out of trouble. For many of us, this behavior adaptability is a habit rather than a conscious decision.

We can choose our behaviors and, by doing so, make our relationships more effective.   Very often we behave out of habit and use behaviors that are within our comfort zone. Many people believe their behavior is limited by their childhood experiences or controlled by other people. How often have you heard someone say, "That's just the way I am." or "What else could I do, after what he did?" The truth is, we can choose our behaviors and adapt or modify our styles to meet the needs of the situation and other people. The questions for many people then becomes, "Why should I do that? Didn't Shakespeare say 'To thine own self be true'?"

Choosing Behaviors and Adapting Your Style

If you want to adapt your behavioral style, you have to be willing to try behaviors that you may not feel comfortable with and you have to have the behavioral skills within your behavior repertoire. Alessandra and O'Connor call this behavioral flexibility and versatility. An unwillingness to adapt is often based on a belief that it involves giving up personal power.

Some people believe that when they adapt their behavior they are selling out and not being themselves. This is often because they are looking at the relationship as a win-lose situation: If I change the way I act to meet your needs, that must mean you win and I lose. Looking at relationships this way can lead to ego games and power trips. I don't want to adapt to your style, so I rub you the wrong way and you become even more determined that your way is the right way. Unless someone "gives in" and adapts, the result is a damaged relationship - and possibly lost business.

Look at it as a win-win situation and you'll see that you can adapt your behavior based on your needs as well as the needs of the other person. The easiest way to do this is to focus on the relationship rather than on looking at the people involved as potential winners or losers. Look at what it will take to make the relationship a success (the needs of the relationship). Then choose your behaviors and adapt your style to also fit with your needs and the needs of the other person. The result is rapport and a good relationship and a win-win situation for everyone involved.

Looking at it another way, suppose Fred and Ginger want to dance but neither really enjoys dancing backward. For the sake of the dance, one of them will do so. Probably Ginger, since she really wants to dance - just as you want to do business with your client. She also knows that by the very nature of the dance, Fred will dance backward at some point (although not in high heels!) and they'll both have an opportunity to face the audience and do their thing. In addition, some of Ginger's moves while dancing backward will naturally and easily lead Fred into dancing backward. Because of all this, the dance is successful and both Fred and Ginger feel successful and satisfied with what happens.

Some people don't have a problem "dancing backward" or adapting their style. They are, however, concerned when they make a move that causes Fred to begin dancing backward. Since that is not his usual preference, it must mean he is being manipulated!

Adapting your style is not manipulative behavior. You do it all the time. You wear certain clothes in certain situations to influence other people's opinions of you. Depending on wind and course conditions, you choose a different club and use a different strategy to influence the results. You are doing basically the same thing when you adapt your behavior within a relationship.

Fear of being manipulative is based on the win-lose model. Think in terms of win-win and you'll see you are not being manipulative. You are treating the person as they prefer to be treated. And you are working toward meeting the needs of the other person, the relationship, and your own needs as well.

Choosing your behavior based on your knowledge of someone else's style is just a variation of how most of us behave most of the time anyway. We act, get feedback from others, and modify our actions based on that feedback. But we're actually *reacting* - and usually only when the feedback is loud and strong enough to get us to start listening.

When we choose our behavior based on an understanding of a behavior model, we become proactive. We are looking much more carefully at all the information we have available about the person. We are making much more effective use of the feedback and we are choosing our behavior accordingly. But to do this, we need to know how to read people. This means not only being more observant, but also processing the information we collect and using it to adapt our style.

How to Read People

We learn about other people from what they say, how they say it, how they act - everything about them. In a famous study, Albert Mehrabian concluded that communication is 8 percent verbal (the actual words we choose); 37 percent vocal (the way we say it, our tone of voice, volume, pace of speaking, inflection, and vocal variety); and 55 percent visual and nonverbal (our body language). Pick up clues about someone by noticing the words they choose, how quickly they talk, and how they use their voice.

Pay special attention to the nonverbal or visual clues they are giving you: their gestures and mannerisms, walk, eye contact, and facial expressions. Also take note of how they interact with their environment. How do they organize their space? What does the decor and their choice and attitude toward possessions tell you?

Take all the information you observed and think about how it applies to the behavioral model. Do the behaviors reflect someone who is people-oriented (a Socializer or a Relater) or someone who is task-oriented (a Director or a Thinker)? Are they fast-paced and direct (Directors and Socializers) or more laid back (Relaters and Thinkers)? This process will give you a general feel for the person's style. Continue observing and collecting information. Make your behavior choices based on everything you know about the person, on and off the course, and about the preferences of people who have a similar style.

Business Golf With the Four Behavioral Styles

Let's look at the four behavioral styles in terms of what you *might* observe about someone and what your behavior choices *could* be.

The Director

In the office you may observe:

- Fast-paced individual who is bottom line, results-oriented.
- An aura of authority, power, and success in terms of possessions, office decor, interactions with others.
- Constant activity, concern with time.
- No nonsense, get-to-the-point conversation style.
- Self-assured tone of voice. Speaks with authority.
- Confident posture, broad use of gestures. Strong handshake, good eye contact.
- Likes to be in control, win, take credit.
- Brusque with people.

On the golf course you may observe:

- Large, pro-style bag with expensive, perhaps custom-made clubs.
- Serious attitude toward the game and a determination to win.

- Little chit chat. To-the-point conversation about golf and maybe business.
- Little patience, especially in stressful situations. Hates slow play.
- Competitive. Enjoys side games and wagering.
- Loves the challenges the game presents.
- Takes risks. Will attempt to hit it over the water rather than take a conservative approach and waste a shot.

Possible ways to adapt your behavior:

- Focus more on the game and less on socializing.
- Keep up a fast pace.
- Be open to their suggestions.
- Be decisive in your game (don't dawdle over your strategy) and your language. Avoid using a lot of qualifiers or wishy-washy language.
- If you are a low handicap golfer, carefully read the clues you are getting. Is the Director enjoying the challenge of playing with someone who is skilled or does she have a really strong need to win? You may decide you want to play "customer golf."
- If you are the host:
  1. Be prepared with all the information when you extend the invitation, but give only the essentials. For example, ask, "Are you familiar with the course?" and go from there, rather than giving all the details on how to get there, where the pro shop is located, and so forth.
  2. Make sure all the activities, including the 19th hole, are acceptable to them.
  3. Directors like to be in control. You may want to give them some options to choose from regarding the day's activities. But don't come off sounding indecisive.
  4. They often prefer to bring their own cars. You may not want to suggest car pooling unless they do.
  5. Keep in mind Directors like a challenge. Pick the course accordingly.
  6. Directors are fast-paced and results-oriented. They may prefer playing in a twosome, if the course allows it.
  7. Plan the foursome carefully. Directors don't have much patience for someone who doesn't play well or doesn't know the game. They get along well socially with other Directors, and with Socializers who can focus on the task and control the amount of chit chat. They can get impatient with Thinkers' slow pace and focus on details.

The Socializer

In the office you may observe:

- Outgoing, talkative individual who shows emotion, talks in terms of feelings, and connects with people.
- Not very detail-oriented; speaks in generalities rather than specific facts and figures.
- Vocal variety.
- High energy level; enthusiasm.
- Strong handshake, good eye contact, lots of gestures, variety of facial expressions.
- Not well organized.
- Easily accessible.

On the golf course you may observe:

- Visiting with everyone in the clubhouse.
- Willing to talk about personal matters.
- Likes side games because they add to the fun.
- May have the newest gadgets and equipment.
- Enjoys telling stories and entertaining others.
- Overly optimistic about abilities - can lead to spontaneous risk-taking.
- Not a lot of pre-shot analysis or focus on the game.

Possible ways to adapt your behavior:

- Don't ask them to keep score.
- Use a warm, upbeat, positive approach.
- Give them recognition both publicly and privately.
- Don't dominate the conversation.
- If you are the host:
  1. Arrange a day that is fun with a 19th hole activity that allows them to meet other people. You may want to consider an outing.
  2. Make suggestions that let them look good.
  3. Socializers may find Thinkers too quiet and reserved and too focused on details. Too many Socializers in a foursome can slow down the game. They can relate well during the 19th hole as long as no one is stealing the spotlight.

The Relater

In the office you may observe:

- Slower paced; laid back, low-keyed individual.
- More reserved use of gestures, facial expression.
- A good listener.
- Cooperative; a team player.
- Prefers a few close relationships rather than more casual interacting with a large group.
- Prefers staying within their comfort zone.

On the golf course you may observe:

- Tolerant of behavior of others; patient.
- Pleasant; out for a good day regardless of anything else.
- Happy for others' success; urges others on; tries to calm excited players down.
- Predictable; not heavily into course management. Often plays one preferred course in the same way with the same choice of clubs.
- Focuses on the game, but also enjoys talking with others.

Possible ways to adapt your behavior:

- Recognize them privately with very specific feedback since they don't like the spotlight.
- Avoid confrontation.
- Use a casual, easy-going approach.
- If you are the host:
  1. They may prefer a course they know.
  2. Give them step-by-step information. Get their input.
  3. Familiarize them with a new course. Plan the day and discuss it with them rather than being spontaneous.
  4. Don't plan a 19th hole activity that might infringe on their personal life and time unless you get their okay first.
  5. They may prefer to car pool.
  6. They may enjoy playing with people they already know.
  7. They relate well to all the styles, but some Directors and Socializers may find Relaters too laid back and slow-paced.

The Thinker

In the office you may observe:

- Neat, very organized.
- Reserved, formal, keep their distance.
- Cool handshake.
- Slower paced, very methodical.
- Brief and to the point; uses facts and figures and thinking words.

On the golf course you may observe:

- Enjoys keeping score.
- A stickler for the rules.
- Focuses on performance.
- Very neat, methodical with equipment and in the locker room.
- Not very involved with others in the foursome.
- Focuses on details, accuracy of each shot.

Possible ways to adapt your behavior:

- Watch their body language carefully for clues, since they don't say much.
- Be formal, polite, and respect their need for space.
- Focus on their efforts (their setup, swing, course management) as well as on the results.
- Carefully follow the rules.
- Use a logical approach to your game rather than taking risks.
- If you are the host:
  1. Give them all the details.
  2. Avoid abrupt changes to the plans.
  3. Discuss the course with them.
  4. They'll probably enjoy playing with Relaters and other Thinkers.
  5. Since they aren't "talkers," mention common interests when you introduce them to people.
  6. When you plan the 19th hole activity, remember they prefer small groups that they feel comfortable with.

Putting it All in Perspective

Of course you'll meet people in each of the behavioral styles who'll send you very different clues and who will be harder to read. You may decide that based on your own style and what you know about the person, you don't feel comfortable adapting your behavior according to the suggestions. This will happen because we are only considering the person's basic behavioral tendencies. Since we're all a blend of the various styles, we also have to look at the secondary tendencies (just as we did for Arnold Palmer and Fuzzy Zoeller).

When we consider two behavioral styles, about 95 percent of the population fall into one of sixteen patterns. *People Smarts* explains this in more detail and includes an inventory to help you determine your own pattern. Knowing the sixteen patterns will give you greater insight into the clues that behavior gives about the goals and fears that motivate us all. See the Resource Section for more information on *People Smarts*.

This chapter has been a brief introduction to the four behavioral styles. Giving you more detailed information here would be like explaining all fourteen clubs at your first golf lesson. But learning the difference between the irons and woods, between the driver and the putter (between the four behavioral styles) gives you the basic information you need to get started. If you'd like to learn more about your own on course style, you can do so with *The Golfer's Profile*. See the Resource Section for more information on this valuable tool.

Using the basic behavioral model will give you a greater understanding of your own behavior and insight into how others behave. You'll become more observant of the clues others give you about how they prefer to be treated. You'll also begin to rely less on your own behavioral habits. When you make conscious choices about your behavior, you can build on your strengths and work on what hasn't been serving you well.

The golf course is a great place to polish your skills in using the model. As mentioned in Chapter 1, eighteen holes give you plenty of time to see people in many situations, and you can really get to know them. But you have to know how to read the clues they are giving you and act accordingly. It is certainly worth the effort. Give it a try. You'll notice a difference in your effectiveness and in the quality of your relationships, both on and off the golf course.

Summary

Your success in business golf depends on how well you can establish rapport and develop relationships with other people. Knowing how to read people and understand their behavior as well as your own is a critical part of this. Behavioral models can simplify the process of sorting through all the information and feedback you receive from others. It can also help you identify your own style so you can adapt behaviors that are more effective.

How to Keep the Coversation in Play
Small Talk on the Golf Course

Chi Chi Rodriguez, who joined the PGA Tour in 1960, the Senior PGA Tour in 1985, and represented Puerto Rico on twelve World Cup teams, is about as well known for his humanitarian efforts, colorful personality, and quick wit as for his super shots. He has joked that even after many years on the tour, his accent still creates communication problems that embarrass him. He says he once asked his caddie for a sand wedge and the caddie came back ten minutes later with a ham on rye!

Although an accent can be a challenge to good communication, I doubt if it was ever a real problem for Chi Chi. He has a way of reaching people's ears, funny bones, and hearts. But all of us have experienced some sort of challenge in our communication. For some of us, it may happen on a regular basis; for others, perhaps only with certain people.

When this happens on the golf course during a round of business golf, it can be just as intimidating as the bunkers and water hazards. You handle the physical barriers the course architects designed by planning your game around them. You also develop the skill to deal with them because you know you'll eventually have to. You can use the same kind of strategy to keep the conversation ball in play. Course management skills are critical to your success in golf. Conversation management skills are just as critical to your success in business golf.

The Special Challenges of On-Course Conversation

Even people who have mastered the art of small talk and are gifted conversationalists in business social situations find they often have to adapt their skills to meet the special demands of business golf conversation. There are several reasons for this.

The extended time frame

It is hard to think of any other social business activity that puts you in close proximity to such a limited number of people for such a long period of time. You can't mix and mingle and play the social butterfly, a technique many people use at business parties when conversation becomes difficult. You can't seek temporary relief with a group of friends, the way many others deal with business social events. You can't even excuse yourself to go to the restroom, the ploy you might use if you hit the conversation doldrums or wanted to rethink your strategy during a business lunch. No wonder so many people have an anxiety attack if they have to play with their boss or an important client.

When you head out for a round of business golf, you really have to know that you can handle any situation and project a confident image over an extended period of time, because you never know what might happen during the round.

The ups and downs that occur during a round

At most business-related events we know what to expect and how people will behave. The situation is usually pretty stable and not emotionally demanding. During a round of golf, however, a player will face many challenges and probably experience a series of highs and lows. You have to deal with other people's emotions as well as your own. Knowing what to say and how to handle various situations takes special skill. You also need to know when to shift your focus from golf and golf-related conversation to other topics.

Maintaining the balance between conversation and golf

The dynamics of business golf are much different than the dynamics of most other business social activities because golf is a complex task that requires a great deal of concentration. You can, for example, easily have a conversation over a business lunch because the task of eating doesn't demand a lot of your attention.

But have you ever met a business associate for lunch and had so much to talk about that you immediately focused your full attention on the conversation? You haven't even thought about lunch when the waiter comes to take the order. You completely forgot the task at hand while you were focusing on the conversation. You immediately shift your attention to the menu and with one quick glance, select something (anything!) so you can get back to the important stuff - the conversation. And what often happens? One of you probably says something like, "Now where were we?" You then have to reconstruct the conversation and possibly work a bit to regain the momentum and enthusiasm you had before the waiter forced you to change your focus.

When you really look at the dynamics of the situation, you see that you didn't focus on the task at hand (food selection) because you were too involved in the conversation. When the task finally demanded your attention, it became an interruption to the conversation. So you gave it less time and attention than you usually would. The result may have affected the quality and enjoyment of both the conversation and the lunch.

Hitting a golf ball is a much more complex task than ordering lunch. It requires your full concentration - before, during, and just after each shot. Consider how many shots you hit during an average round and you appreciate the special challenges of business golf. And when you play in a foursome, the focus between the conversation and the task of someone hitting a shot will shift several hundred times!

This special challenge requires the skill of moving from task to talk and back again while staying focused throughout. It is "putting yourself in a bubble," ala Seve Ballesteros, when you are hitting a shot. This requires totally focusing on your game and blocking out thoughts and emotions generated by the earlier conversation, and then moving back into the conversation with ease.

The amount and focus of the conversation will depend on the individuals in your foursome. You'll adapt your conversation to the foursome just as you'll adapt your golf game based on the course and course conditions. In course management, you plan your strategy in advance and then modify it according to what actually happens during the round. Manage your conversation in much the same way.

Conversation Management Tips

There are five conversation management tips. They are:
1. Focus on your objectives.
2. Have the conversation skills to reach your objectives.
3. List what you already know about the other person.
4. Develop a specific strategy.
5. Be flexible.

Focus on Your Objectives

Whatever your ultimate business objective, you need a conversation strategy that will help you develop trust as you get to know the other person and allow them to get to know you. These are the basic objectives of all business golf.

Develop trust by creating rapport and building a relationship.
Whether you are playing with someone you've known for a while or going
out alone to network, this is your number one objective and it may very
well lead to business. Unless you do this, you won't reach any other
business objective you may have.

This is the cornerstone of business golf because people tend to do
business with people they know, like, trust, and perceive as being like
themselves. The title of Harvey Penick's book, *And If You Play Golf You
Are My Friend*, rings true for a lot of people. The fact that you play golf
gives you a common denominator to build on. Developing rapport and
working on the relationship is the next logical step. You do this by communicating with each other, verbally and nonverbally. Through a
balanced, two-way interaction that combines listening and sharing information, you get to know the other person and let them get to know you.

Get to know the other person. You can do this through active listening and by moving the conversation toward topics that interest the other
person. This involves focusing on the other person rather than on yourself.

People who have difficulty starting a conversation and keeping it
going are often focused inward. They are thinking of their own agenda and
objectives, what they'll say next, how they look. While they are doing this,
they miss the nonverbal clues the other person is giving them. They also
fail to pick up the clues in what the other person says and what is
happening around them. They are missing all the raw material they could
use to keep the conversation going. We all do this from time to time. No
wonder conversations are sometimes strained!

When you focus on others, you send the message that they are
important. People tend to respond to this and will open up more quickly
and let you get to know them. They will also often focus more on you.
Rapport is developed much more quickly this way.

Let the other person get to know you.   Although getting to know
the other person may seem more important in helping you tailor your
product or service to meet their needs, letting them get to know you is just
as critical in developing a good business relationship. It is difficult to
develop trust unless the other person has a good sense of who you are on
a business and personal level. When you share your interests and talk
about what is important to you, you also give the person an idea about
your values and attitudes. This is what helps the other person decide if
they want to do business with you.

Sharing information about yourself is vital in keeping the two-way
exchange balanced. Appropriate self-disclosure really helps move the
relationship ahead.

Have fun! Always make sure you are going out to have fun. Relax and enjoy yourself. If you don't plan to have fun, you may as well stay in the office because your attitude will reflect how you feel and create a barrier to good communication. When you are relaxed and enjoying yourself, you'll be more fun to be around. Again, rapport will develop more quickly.

I was amazed how many teaching pros told me stories about people who came in for lessons because "they had to for business." During the lessons, the pros could tell that these people would rather be somewhere else. Their hearts weren't in it. This is very different than learning to play because you know golf is a valuable business tool. It may be only a matter of attitude, but your attitude can spell the difference between success and failure in business golf. One attitude is negative. It is a bite-the-bullet, "I don't wanna, but I gotta" feeling that comes off to others as condescending. The other is a positive approach that shows respect for the game and those who love it. With the positive approach, you can have fun and enjoy yourself even if golf isn't your favorite pastime. And when you are having fun and being yourself, conversation is much easier.

Stay in the moment and make it a point to enjoy what you are doing at that moment. When it is your turn to play, focus on the game. When you talk with others, focus on them and the conversation. If and when you do business, focus on business. Focusing will help you find something to enjoy about each activity and will add to your success. It will also help you master the art of business golf small talk.

Have the Conversation Skills to Reach Your Objectives

To feel really comfortable with business golf small talk, you have to feel secure with your conversation skills in general. If you are usually uncomfortable initiating or keeping a conversation going, you'll find Don Gabor's books *How to Start a Conversation and Make Friends* and *Speaking Your Mind in 101 Difficult Situations* helpful. Whatever your skill level, you'll benefit from his free tip sheet on "50 Ways to Improve Your Conversations." (See the Resource Section.) It provides a lot of valuable ideas you can use both on and off the course.

During the round, you can lower your conversation handicap if you become more aware of nonverbal communication, use active listening skills, share appropriately, and know when to keep silent.

Be aware of nonverbal communication, your own and others. As mentioned in the last chapter, a major portion of all communication is non-verbal. It takes on even more significance in business golf because so much time is spent on the task of golf. You must pay attention to the body language of others, not only during conversation but also when they play.

Although you can learn a lot about a person by watching how they play, you can often learn even more by observing how they *react* to how they and others play. Look at their facial expressions during the setup, consider their gestures just after they've completed the shot. Notice their posture and how they walk. As Ben Crenshaw once told *Golf Digest*, "You can tell by the way a guy walks how he's doing." It may not tell you a person's skill level, but body language does say a lot about how someone is *reacting* to how they are playing.

If golf reveals true character, as so many people say, it is revealed more through the nonverbal than through conversation. The conversation paints a picture of who the person is, but the nonverbal, especially around the task of golf, adds color and dimension to it by giving us clues about the person's feelings, beliefs, and values.

Don't miss the opportunity to pick up on these clues. It is this information that will tell you how important the game is to the person. It will also help you decide where to go with the conversation. Is silence appropriate? Would this person respond better to a brief comment or a lengthier conversation about the shot and course conditions? Is it time to move from the topic of golf back into regular conversation?

When business is lost on the golf course, it is usually because someone is unaware of the nonverbal messages they are receiving or sending. If you don't read the clues, you may bring up business too soon and damage the rapport you've established. Or you may wait too long and miss a chance to introduce a business-related topic and lay the ground work for further discussion. If you practice focusing more on other people's body language, it will help you avoid these mistakes.

Even more business may be lost through the nonverbal messages you send to others. Our body language can communicate character traits (impatience, lack of confidence, dishonesty) that are undesirable and are not congruent with our verbal messages. We can unconsciously paint a picture of ourselves as someone the other person would not want to do business with.

Develop an awareness of the nonverbal messages you are sending. Asking a friend for feedback during a recreational round is a great way to do this. Learn to adapt your nonverbal communication just as you would your conversation style. It can make the difference between success and failure in business golf.

Someone once said we've been given two eyes, two ears, but only one mouth, and the wise person uses them in that proportion. The first tip for successful business golf conversation involved using your eyes to observe. Before we look at what we can say on the golf course, let's focus on how we can get the most from what we hear.

Use active listening skills, which involves really focusing on the other person and the conversation. Have you ever been in a classroom or meeting and suddenly realized that you were a million miles away and didn't know what had just been said? This happens to us all because we focus on ourselves. Something is said that impacts us and our thoughts stay with that idea or go off on a tangent. Or we focus on ourselves by wondering what we can say next, so we're thinking instead of listening. The sound waves may reach our ears, but because our brains are otherwise engaged, we really don't hear. Then something is said that focuses us back on the conversation - a question directed at us or perhaps a comment that catches our interest.

This in-and-out style of listening makes conversation very difficult. We feel uncomfortable and on the spot and don't know what to say. In business, this kind of listening causes us to miss important information and clues about the other person and how we can best serve them. Unfortunately, this type of listening is very prevalent on the golf course because it is so easy to focus on the task of golf when we should be focused on the conversation.

Work to develop your active listening for business golf. Because a great deal of the conversation will take place while you are riding in a golf cart or walking down the fairway, you won't be able to rely as much on the body language of active listening - smiling, nodding, making eye contact, and using open gestures. Therefore, it is even more important to carefully concentrate on the words that are said (the verbal) and how they are said (vocal variety). This active listening will help you move the conversation along more easily. It will also help you remember important information for future reference. As you listen, pay special attention to the following:

- **Hot topics.** Listen for topics that generate enthusiasm and interest in the other person. What turns them on? What are their interests and passions? You can get this information by asking questions, but also by listening carefully to free information they give you while talking about other topics. The more hot topics and interests you have in common, the easier it is to establish rapport, develop the relationship, and build trust.
- **Key information.** As you listen, you will hear a lot of information that you can use to move the conversation in a certain direction, to change the topic, or to file for future reference. Let's say you are talking about great courses you've played, and your partner says, "Last year when I was in California checking out colleges for my son, a business associate invited me to play Torrey Pines.

What a great course!" You'd probably stay with this hot topic and ask a question about Torrey Pines.

With active listening, you pick up all the additional key information you hear, make a mental note to remember it, and file it for future use. The next topic could be California. You also know there's a college-aged son. During the 19th hole you could steer the conversation toward business by saying something like, "You mentioned playing Torrey Pines with a business associate. Does your company do a lot of business in California?"

Key words and details help you keep the conversation moving. Following up on them helps you build rapport because it shows the other person you are listening and are interested in them.

- **Iceberg statements**. Very often people give us a clue that they have something to say, but like an iceberg, most of it is hidden. It is up to us to pick up the clue and ask a question to let them know we are interested and want to hear about it. Suppose your client says, "I'm really looking forward to playing. I've had *some* morning." By asking, "What happened?" you can open up a hot topic and gather key information. You'll also convey that you are interested and willing to listen to whatever the other person has to say.

  Unless you are actively listening, you can easily miss an iceberg statement. So when you follow up on one, you are perceived as a sensitive and caring person as well as a good listener.

- **Cues to talking business.** Within the hot topics, key information, and iceberg statements, you'll hear cues to business-related topics. Listen very carefully for them, make a special mental note of them, and plan to use the information at an appropriate time.

  When you actively listen, remember, and use the information you've heard, you'll find the conversation becomes an easy give-and-take, two-way exchange. But what if the other person doesn't have much to say and you end up with most of the responsibility for keeping the conversation going. What can you say for four-plus hours?

Know the role of business talk.   When people are uncomfortable with business golf small talk, it is usually because they don't know what to talk about or don't know if and when to talk business. Developing a conversation strategy and using active listening skills will help you know what to talk about. If you are in doubt about business talk, keep these points in mind.

Talking business is not the same as *doing business.* You can discuss business in general without touching on the subject of how you and your company can benefit the other person. The iceberg statement above is a perfect example of this. When you ask, "What happened?" the other person may give you a lot of information about what is happening in her company. This could start a conversation about local economic conditions, the cyclical nature of business, or market trends. You would not use this opportunity to go into a sales pitch about how your product or service could solve all the problems. Instead, you'd mentally file this key information and use it at a more appropriate time.

Talking business at the wrong time can damage the relationship. Let's assume again that your playing partner says, "Last year when I was in California checking out colleges for my son, a business associate invited me to play Torrey Pines. What a great course!" It would be inappropriate to respond with, "Do you do a lot of business in California?" The round at Torrey Pines is a hot topic that your partner would enjoy talking about. If you steer the conversation to business, you'll communicate that you either didn't sense that this was important to him or didn't care. It could also send the message that you are manipulative and only interested in doing business.

Later in the round or during the 19th hole, you could introduce the topic of business. It is not the topic that's inappropriate, but the timing of it.

Keep in mind that talking business can build your business image. Although most of us prefer to do business with someone we know and like, we also want to be sure that person is competent. If you avoid picking up on business-related cues, you can send the message that you aren't very knowledgeable. Talking intelligently about business in general helps build your image as a capable business person. It also establishes more common ground and helps build a stronger foundation for the relationship. So don't be afraid to talk business. But if you are in doubt about the appropriateness, it is best to wait and bring it up later.

Know that silence is a normal part of a good conversation.   It is also an *essential* part of conversation on the golf course, because talking while anyone's playing is a major breach of etiquette. Don't be concerned about occasional lulls in the conversation. They give everyone time to think about what has been said, focus on the beautiful environment, and possibly think of new topics to introduce.

When you have a need for constant conversation, you are really communicating your anxiety about the situation. This doesn't help your business golf image. So use occasional silence to your advantage, knowing that if it becomes more than occasional or really awkward, you are prepared to get the conversation going again. You'll have a lot of topics you can talk about if you learn as much about the person beforehand as you can.

List What You Already Know About the Other Person

To help you develop possible topics of conversation and a conversation strategy, you'll want to know as much about the other person as you can. Develop a list of what you know and do research, if necessary. You may have already started a list of this type, because it can be a great sales and customer service tool. Harvey Mackay discusses this in *Swim With the Sharks Without Being Eaten Alive*, and has developed the "Mackay 66" questionnaire to help organize the process of collecting information about your business associates. If this process is new to you, you'll find Mackay's book helpful. (See the Resource Section.) Don't overlook this important step of gathering information about your business associate. It can be a very powerful tool.

Be sure to include everything you know about them, whether it is golf-related or not. Consider their behavioral style, how serious they are about golf (their archetype), and what you've observed about them in the past. If you don't have much information, you may want to talk to mutual associates or in some other way research the person. To start the process, ask yourself the following questions:

What is the person's behavior style? Think about and observe the person in terms of the behavioral styles discussed in the last chapter. Is she more task-oriented or people- and relationship-oriented? Is he fast-paced and direct or more laid back? Even if you can't immediately identify a behavioral style, asking yourself these questions will help you focus more on the other person and become more observant. Knowing the behavioral style will give you some ideas about how to handle the conversation and how to adapt your own style.

Task-oriented individuals (Directors and Thinkers) will probably find too much conversation a distraction. They prefer to focus on the game. A large part of their conversation may be golf-related. Because Directors are more direct and fast-paced, they adapt well to the snippets style of conversation that takes place during a round. You'll want to avoid too much chit chat and long, drawn out stories. If you are relationship oriented (a Socializer or a Relater), this may mean modifying your style somewhat.

Thinkers are usually slower paced and often more concerned with all the details of the game. Because they are so focused on the game and often not very outgoing, you may find it difficult to draw them into a conversation. Golf-related topics are an easy way to get them involved. But respect their need to focus intently on the game.

If you are out with a relationship-oriented individual (Socializers and Relaters) and you are also relationship-oriented, you'll probably have no problems getting the conversation going (especially if you are both Socializers!). In this case, you may have to work to keep the conversation in check. Socializers often enjoy telling and listening to anecdotal stories. They are often more willing to share information about their feelings and personal life. Relaters tend to be good listeners. Get a group of relationship-oriented people on the golf course and they could easily slow down play. Especially if they are not serious golfers. Here you would adapt your style to focus more on the game and you would save the lengthy conversation for the 19th hole.

If you are both task-related, there might not be much conversation at all and most of it may be golf-related. You can still develop rapport and build the relationship because you are sharing a common experience. In this case, the nonverbal communication becomes even more important because verbal communication is so limited. You'll still want to have a good list of possible topics because the major responsibility for keeping the conversation going will be yours.

How serious is the person about golf? To determine this, find out how long she has been playing. How often does he play? What is his handicap? Does she belong to a club? Has he won any tournaments or played in any pro-ams? Do you think he is a Gunslinger, Non-Competitor, Escapist or Power Player?

Knowing the person's golf archetype can tell you how serious they are about the game. Knowing this will help you reach the right balance between conversation and golf. As a rule, serious golfers (Escapists, Power Players, and Gunslingers) prefer to focus more on playing and less on conversation.

Your observations about the person as well as any information you can get from others or through research will help you develop a list of topics you can discuss.

What have you observed about the other person and what do you already know about them? (This is where the "Mackay 66" can be a big help.) Think of and list everything you know about the person: where she works, her occupation, any facts you have from previous conversations. Think about his office. What is it like? Did you see a picture of his family or an award hanging on the wall? A diploma? Where did he go to school? What organization gave the award and for what reason?

Get any information you can about the person from others. Add this to your list. Make your list as complete as possible. Then start to plan your strategy by analyzing the list. Ask yourself what each item tells you about the other person's experiences and interests and what possible topics of conversation relate to that.

For example, if you saw a family picture taken on a sailboat, you might have added, "married, two teenaged sons, enjoys sailing," to your list. From this list, come up with possible topics - children, sailing. Then use your imagination to come up with other topics that are related but may be one or two steps removed. These topics could include family vacations, sports that their children are involved in, kinds of music teenagers enjoy, college selection, where the person learned to sail, a cruise a friend of yours took, or the types of vacations you enjoy.

Do this for each item on the list until you have at least a dozen or more topics you could talk about with this person. *Think in terms of finding their hot topics and linking them to hot topics of your own.* Also think about how you might make each of these topics more than casual chit chat about activities. *Is there a way to weave your attitudes and values about life and business into the topic so the other person can get to know you on a deeper level?*

For example, if we are talking about sports and hobbies, I might say that I really enjoy my new home because it is located so close to the golf courses and bike and hiking trails at the state park. I might add that it was the sense of community that exists in the village as well as the school system that really made me choose the area. From this, the other person learns that I am concerned about physical fitness, value education, and may be involved in community activities. It might also indicate that I make decisions after considering all the details. In a few sentences, I've told the person not only about sports and hobbies I enjoy, but have also given a sense of who I am as a person, what I value, and maybe even how I do business. This is the kind of information that lets people really get to know us. So as you develop your list, think about how your possible topics relate to your attitudes and values.

Review your list and do any research necessary so you'll feel comfortable talking about each topic. This may mean reading some newsmagazines or the sports or business section of a newspaper you may not normally read. Once you feel comfortable with the topics, you can develop your strategy.

Develop a Specific Strategy

When you pick up a scorecard in the pro shop, you look at the course layout and begin to think about course management. Sometimes in the pro shop you'll see a special sign posted that warns you of conditions that will influence your play. In Florida, it may be, "Beware of alligators." In the Northeast, it may be a warning about ticks and the dangers of Lyme Disease. This information is something to keep in mind during the entire round.

Before you plan your conversation strategy, think about the conversation dangers that have been known to get business golfers in trouble, and keep them in mind throughout the entire round. Some conversation hazards to avoid are:

1. Don't talk too much.
2. Don't bring up business too soon.
3. Don't disclose personal information such as family problems.
4. Don't talk about other clients.
5. Don't talk about confidential business matters.
6. Don't give unsolicited advice about golf.
7. Don't say anything negative about the course if you are the guest.
8. Don't talk about other players.
9. Don't ask so many questions that you seem rude or nosy.
10. Don't let your emotions get in the way. Think before you speak.

With these hazards in mind, plan your conversation strategy on paper. You may not use the exact strategy you plan, just as you'll change your golf strategy based on how you are hitting the ball. But unless you plan in a structured way, you probably won't cover all the possibilities that may come up.

In course management, you begin on the tee and plan your shots to take you down the fairway, to the green, and into the hole. You note the rough and hazards and have some idea of how you would handle meeting those challenges. Plan your conversation strategy in exactly the same way. Think of the total picture.

Let's say setting up a follow-up appointment to talk business is your ultimate business objective for the round. Think of that as the equivalent of getting the ball in the hole. Exactly what do you need to do to get there? Plan a possible conversation opener (your tee shot), several possible follow-up topics to move the relationship along toward your goal (fairway shots), business-related topics (the chip shots that get you on the green), and the topics that will result in you getting the appointment (putting out). Also think about how you would handle special situations such as dealing with someone's temper tantrum, cheating, or non-stop talking (the bunkers and water hazards).

Plan your strategy to reach your objective, even though you know you'll modify it based on the give-and-take and spontaneous nature of good conversation. The topics you planned are like the fourteen clubs in your bag. You may not use them all and you'll probably use ones you didn't think you would. But you'll be prepared and it is this preparation that will lead you to success.

The conversation opener - the tee shot. As you arrive at the course and prepare to play the round, golf and golf-related topics will probably dominate the conversation. Somewhere during the first hole someone will often shift the conversation to a non-golf topic. However, as each shot is played, it is fairly common to talk about the shot as a way to make the transition back into conversation. Brief conversation snippets are typical on the golf course, so many people prefer to save important topics, including business, until the 19th hole.

Keeping the conversation going - moving down the fairway. Think of the topics you could introduce and how they fit into your overall strategy. Try to arrange your topics so the conversation naturally flows toward your objective. Work at building a momentum that moves the conversation away from superficial topics (such as the weather) toward topics that will really help the relationship develop. Discuss business-related topics when the other person brings them up or when you sense the time is right.

Handling difficult situations — getting out of the rough or the hazard. Suppose you are out with your boss and after a few bad shots, he begins throwing clubs and swearing - or even cheating. Or your client is a know-it-all expert who is constantly giving you pointers and criticizing your game. Or a member of the foursome that you just met is not only an inept golfer, but also insists on talking endlessly. How can you handle situations such as these?

The first thing to do is to refocus on your objectives. Remember you are playing business golf and your basic objective involves developing rapport and building a relationship. Ask yourself how you can handle the situation and still meet your objectives. Answering this question will help put the behavior in perspective and also give you time to think and develop a strategy rather than reacting emotionally.

You may decide to ignore the behavior for the sake of the relationship. Or you may find the behavior so offensive to your personal values that you decide you don't want a business relationship with this person. You also could choose to deal with the situation without damaging the other person's self-esteem or the relationship. To do this, you'll need some guidelines that will help you deal with any difficult situation. These are:

1. Stay emotionally detached, if possible.
2. Empathize with the other person.
3. Don't attack the other person.
4. Keep it light. Don't make a big issue out of it.
5. Think before you speak.
6. Humor can often help, as long as it isn't sarcastic.
7. Keep your vocal qualities (tone, pitch, pace) friendly.

Let's look at a few examples of possible ways to deal with some difficult situations.

- **Cheating.** This is probably the toughest one. Depending on the relationship, many people will just ignore the behavior. (Would you call your boss on cheating?) When you empathize, you may come to the conclusion that the person really needs to win. So you may decide customer golf is appropriate. Or you may decide the person isn't cheating. Maybe they are new and don't really know the rules. If the person moves the ball to a better lie, you might say something like, "Do you want to play winter rules?" (Winter rules permit moving the ball to improve the lie). But make sure it doesn't sound sarcastic.

    In the Hyatt Study, less than half (45 percent) of the executives who played with someone who cheated confronted the player about it. Because it is so difficult to call a person on it without damaging their self-esteem and the relationship, think very carefully before you deal with the situation. If you do decide to confront the player, make sure it is in private and not in front of the other members of the foursome.

- **The Complainer.** Again, empathize. Sometimes the person doesn't realize they are complaining so much. Other times, they may be looking for encouragement and seeking sympathy. Let the person know you heard what they said, but don't encourage them to complain even more. For example, if they are complaining about their swing, don't ask a question such as, "Is it this particular course or do you have a tendency to slice it?" You might say something like, "This game can get to anybody. I find that if I just let it go, I usually do better on the next shot. Like they say, the game's 90 percent mental." It also often works to refocus the conversation to a non-golf topic.

- **The Expert.** Some people seem to know everything about everything - or at least they think they do! During the round, this often takes the form of unwanted advice about the course or your game. When I empathize, I try to decide if it is their problem or mine. Sometimes, the suggestion is valid and could help, but I get irritated because I'm upset with my game. So the problem is with me.

    But if the person is really becoming a distraction, I might say, "I appreciate your help and I know my game needs some work. My instructor is helping me with it. Right now I need to stay focused and not think about too many things at once." In this case, how you say it is as important as what you say.

- **The Non-Stop Chatterbox.** This may be the most common difficult situation you encounter. As always, empathize to try to understand what is really going on. If the person is new to golf and doesn't know the etiquette, you might say something like, "The setup and swing really require a lot of concentration, so it is important that we don't distract John with our talking."

If the person is carried away with a hot topic, you might say, "That sounds like a great vacation! I'd really like to hear more about it, but it is hard to talk between shots. Let's talk about it over lunch."

You also can use nonverbal cues to disengage a chatterbox. Breaking eye contact or turning your head or body toward the person who is addressing the ball can communicate the need for silence.

- **Temper Tantrums**. The usual reason someone throws a tantrum (and possibly a club as well!) is a feeling of frustration over the game. If the person is this angry, it is best to let them express it. Trying to stop a tantrum can result in the anger being directed at you.

Empathize verbally without being condescending. You can often handle this in much the same way you handle a complainer. Say something like, "This game is a challenge even for the pros. But it still beats being back in the office on a beautiful day like this. The next hole has got to be better." If the person is a serious golfer, don't say anything about not being so serious or tell them it is just a game. Focus instead on the opportunity to pull victory from defeat.

These are just a few of the many difficult situations that may come up. Be prepared to deal with them and others if you have to. Keep the general guidelines in mind, be sincere and tactful, and you'll be ready for whatever comes your way.

Moving to business-related topics - getting on the green. You have developed a list of topics, some of which are business-related. You have given some thought to how to strategically present those topics to lead toward a business discussion. Your active listening and interpersonal skills will help you decide on the right time to bring up each topic and if and when to talk business. Always keep your objective in mind. If in doubt about the timing, ask yourself how this might affect the rapport and the relationship you have developed so far.

Achieving your objective - putting out. If your objectives include talking business or setting an appointment, you'll probably include this in your conversation strategy for the 19th hole. Think about how you can make an easy transition from a business-related topic into a casual business discussion. Pay special attention to nonverbal clues and listen actively so you are sure to pick up on whether your timing is right. Chapter 18 focuses on 19th hole conversation in more detail.

Remember that in golf, even though you have planned how you'll play a particular hole, sometimes you may have to pick up (because you are way over par). There's also the possibility that you'll get a hole-in-one, though your chances are about 12,600 to 1. In the same way, even though you have developed a conversation strategy, you may not get to talk about business-related topics at all. Or, on the first hole your client may surprise you and tell you it's a done deal. So whatever your agenda, always keep the final conversation management tip in mind.

Be Flexible

The allure of golf lies in the dynamic nature of the game. Courses vary, course conditions vary, and a very small deviation in your swing can greatly influence the result you get. These challenges require skill, planning, and practice. You also need a variety of tools (clubs) to meet whatever challenge comes your way. Mastering the game involves having the flexibility to adapt to the conditions and knowing when (and when not) to use each club.

The challenge of business golf conversation is much the same. Your conversation depends on the people you are with, how well you know them, and the agenda or strategy they bring to the course. It is dynamic because it will be influenced by the golf experience you are sharing. Although you plan a strategy, you have to remain flexible because you really don't know what the round will bring. Whether or not you follow your strategy, planning for business golf conversation will serve you well. You'll feel more comfortable and self-confident and you'll be more successful in reaching your objectives.

Summary

Business golf conversation can be challenging to even a gifted conversationalist because of the four-to-six hour time frame, the emotional demands of the game, and the need to balance the conversation with the task of playing golf. Planning a conversation strategy is the key to success. Conversation management, much like course management, allows you to progressively move toward your objective of developing the relationship on a personal as well as business level.

Develop a list of possible topics based on what you already know about the other person. Link these topics to interests of your own to help you get to know the other person quickly. Just as important, this will also help the other person get to know you and will help develop a feeling of trust that is a solid foundation for any business relationship.

Because of the dynamic nature of conversation, flexibility is critical. Active listening skills and staying focused on the other person will give you the information to decide if and when to modify your strategy. Take the time to plan your strategy. Whether or not you follow it closely, it will give you the confidence to keep the conversation in play and to reach your business golf objectives.

Does the Golf Course Have a Glass Ceiling
Women and Business Golf

The question of whether or not the golf course has a glass ceiling is really rhetorical. Of course it does. There are very few places where the glass ceiling does not exist. The real question is will the glass ceiling be broken by a golf ball? It may well be.

Increased Interest in Golf as a Business Tool for Women

According to the National Golf Foundation, there are about 6.5 million women golfers in this country, compared to 18 million men. In recent years, however, women accounted for over 40 percent of the 2 million people who took up golf each year. More and more women are recognizing the value of golf as a business tool. Increasingly, corporate America is encouraging women to use it.

Many women told me they were encouraged by their boss to take up golf for business reasons. Several also said golf was discussed as part of the interview process when they were hired, whether it was actually job-related or mentioned as an employee activity. However it was brought up, these women very clearly got the message that knowing how to play was considered a plus in business.

There is a growing trend for corporations to have on-site programs to encourage employees, especially women, to get involved with golf. Anheuser-Busch has included a seminar on golf etiquette and rules as part of its "Women in Business" monthly seminar program. Joan Barcal of *Business Week*, who has played for thirty five years, was instrumental in developing a women's golf school for McGraw-Hill Publishing Co. The program has been so successful that other Manhattan-based companies have enrolled their employees and the school has gone co-ed. Mazda Corporation, recognizing the importance of women in the world of business (52 percent buy cars; 80 percent of the car buying decisions are influenced by women) created the Mazda Golf Clinics for Executive Women to help women develop both business and social skills through golf.

Despite this growing interest, many women are reluctant to learn the game or don't stay with it because they don't have women partners to play with. Nancy Oliver organized golf tournaments for fifteen years but didn't play because she didn't want to learn alone. So in 1991, she set up a golf clinic for women that quickly developed into the Executive Women's Golf League. Since that time, the organization has expanded to over seventy five locations nationwide. Oliver estimates that between 85-90 percent of the women in the league are using golf for business. All the members find the league helpful in developing their skill and in networking with other women golfers. Connecting with other women golfers is becoming less of a problem.

The other major reason women don't get involved with golf is the amount of time required. This problem is not as easy to solve. The time demands on women in business are many and golf does require a major time commitment. The only answer is to weigh the benefits against the cost. Women who use business golf successfully will tell you it is definitely worth the time invested. They'll also tell you there is something else you should be aware of. Once you've found the time and made the commitment, it is still tough for women to use golf as a business tool because of the discrimination that exists against them. The golf course does have a glass ceiling!

Double Standards and Negative Attitudes Against Women

Discrimination against women golfers is coming from so any different directions that someone should yell, "Fore!" when a woman starts out in business golf. The double standard is common at country clubs and golf courses and also in the corporate world. Negative attitudes and gender bias are additional hazards women golfers face.

The Battle of the Sexes

In the Hyatt Study, 36 percent of the women surveyed have experi-enced problems with male golfers, whether playing recreational or busi-ness golf. Almost a third of these women have had to deal with male golfers who were chauvinistic and sexist, and one in five has had to contend with males who did not want to play with women. About 16 percent of the women who experienced problems said these were often ego-related - the men couldn't handle a woman playing well. Other difficulties were due to male impatience or the assumption that women can't play well.

These men may be surprised to learn that women are much more likely than men to take.lessons from a pro - 77 percent of the women compared to just over half of the men. So even if women still haven't mastered the athletic skill, it seems they are at least interested in getting a working knowledge of the game and probably understand the rules and etiquette - which we now know is more important than athletic skill level.

Many men used to excuse their discrimination by saying women slowed down play. Thanks to the research conducted by the National Golf Foundation and publicized by the golf magazines, many men are now aware that women are actually faster players than men. So if you meet a man who is still using this excuse to discriminate, set him straight!

Most of the women I interviewed said they had experienced or were aware of some type of gender bias, but most felt that if they were serious about the game, the men were pretty much willing to give them a chance. And most of the men I talked with said they thought it was great that women were getting into business golf. Many mentioned they even knew some women who were excellent golfers - and a few even said this *without* adding "you know, for a woman."

So although none of the bunkers you run into on the course may be named Archie, chances are you *will* meet some men who have an attitude, however subtle, against women golfers. The best way to deal with it is exactly as you would if it occurred in a business setting and involved a business skill other than golf. Knowing the game and being competent are ways women can change attitudes, but more about that later in the chapter.

Discrimination by Country Clubs and Golf Courses

Because golf has been so closely associated with the old-boy network, it has long been a male-dominated sport. This is very apparent in the rules and restrictions that still exist at the majority of private country clubs where women are openly discriminated against. Because public courses cannot discriminate in this way, the gender bias there is usually more subtle, but nonetheless exists.

Slowly, some private clubs are becoming "gender neutral," by accepting single women as members and giving women voting rights and the same privileges as men. But the by-laws of many private clubs still do not allow a woman to hold club membership. At these clubs, a married woman maintains membership through her husband, but if she is widowed or divorced, she is usually no longer eligible for membership. Of course, these clubs also do not consider unmarried women for membership.

In addition, private clubs often have tee time restrictions that prohibit women from playing before noon or 1:00 PM. These clubs also commonly have restricted access to the restaurant and bar, which, in a stroke of gender-bias genius, is often called The Men's Grill.

Women who have broken the glass ceiling professionally, hold positions of power, or work in male-dominated fields are not exempt from this bias. Three incidents that occurred recently demonstrate the extent of the discrimination.

A Long Island country club with a "males only" policy told their female letter carrier to leave the mail at the gate rather than deliver it to the club house, as the male letter carrier had done. A distinguished New York State Judge was asked to leave another country club where she had been invited to lunch by a colleague. Even one of the most powerful stateswomen was denied access to the restricted dining room!

The "male only" tradition is often even stronger in Europe. An international golf outing coordinator told me he ran into gender bias when he was planning an excursion to the prestigious Prestwick Club, site of the first British Open. Women are allowed to play there only on certain days; the dining room is always "men only."

The outings coordinator met with the club secretary in an attempt to get the rules waived for his client, a major American corporation. The crusty old Scotsman wouldn't hear of it. When asked if he would change the rules for the Queen, he said the Queen was enough of a lady not to ask. She would come on the right day and be happy to be greeted outside!

This kind of discrimination is so blatant that if it existed against any minority or protected group it would result in banner headlines. It creates such a disadvantage for women business golfers that it is in everyone's best interest for all women to work to end it. The National Organization for Women (NOW), the Executive Women's Golf League, and *Golf for Women* magazine are just a few of the organizations that are active in this cause.

More difficult to deal with because we sometimes don't know it exists is the subtle discrimination that is probably more common than we realize and exists at public courses and private clubs that claim not to be restricted. This gender bias was very clearly reported by the ABC-TV news show *Prime Time.*

A young man and a young woman of similar age and backgrounds were sent to shop for a car, apply for a job, and reserve tee times at a public golf course. Gender discrimination existed in all three venues. The man was given a better price on the car and allowed to test drive it alone, while the woman was taken for a ride by the salesman (both literally and price-wise!) The young man was told about and interviewed for management positions, while the woman was only told about secretarial positions at half the salary. At the golf course, he was given his choice of tee times on the two days requested; she was told that only one of the days was open and was given only one available tee time (late afternoon) for that day. The kind of negative publicity this type of program generates can increase awareness about the problem, but unfortunately it will probably take more than this to change the negative attitudes and double standards.

Companies whose employees play business golf can help to end the gender bias by withdrawing their corporate membership from restricted private clubs and their corporate business from public courses. This kind of economic pressure can really bring about changes, but only if companies are willing to do it. Many are not. Although they encourage women to play business golf, they often view it as a less important business skill for women than it is for men.

Mixed Messages From the Corporate Sector

Many of the women I interviewed were encouraged by their employer to get involved in business golf and did so because they recognized it as a helpful business tool and also as the politically correct thing to do. But many also said that within their companies, women business golfers are not taken as seriously as men and often are not given the same opportunities. The perception seems to exist that when men are playing business golf, they are doing business, but when women are playing golf, it is recreational.

A female executive in the financial services industry who is an excellent golfer remains at her desk while her male colleagues often play business golf two or three times a week. She says her boss makes her feel guilty, as though she is goofing off, if she is away from her desk that much. Several women shared with me that they are also receiving the same kind of mixed message: Business golf is good and you should get involved, but do it on your own time.

Oliver believes there is a definite corporate perception that women can't produce business through golf the way men can. She says it is fairly common that companies will pay for men to participate in golf tournaments, but female executives have to participate at their own expense. She suggests documenting the business you develop through golf so you can prove to management that your time on the golf course is well spent. (This is a great idea for men as well.)

Oliver also suggests the buddy system - having several women who are at your skill level and who are also business golfers. This will help fight the frustration and discouragement you'll feel when you are first learning to play or just starting to use it for business purposes. Of course, the Executive Women's Golf League is a great place to find a buddy if you don't already have one!

These suggestions will help women get past the challenges of finding the time, mastering the skill, and dealing with the discrimination. As I said earlier, getting involved in business golf is not as easy for a woman as it is for a man. But as any woman who is a business golfer will tell you, it is definitely worth the effort.

The Importance of Golf as a Business Tool for Women

Now that you have the bad news about the discrimination and negative attitudes women probably have to face, here is the good news: Business golf can be a *more* powerful tool for women than it is for men! Once a woman is a competent golfer, she'll often find that both employer and client perceive her in a very different, much more positive light. This isn't as true for male golfers, because it is assumed that a man will be good! So a good male golfer is perceived as the norm, but a good female golfer is perceived as really special.

A woman business golfer is often not taken seriously unless she has reached a certain skill level, but once she has reached that skill level, she has a greater advantage than the male business golfer. Stated in simple but chauvinistic terms, if you can play golf like a man, they usually assume you are as good as a man.

Many women told me about a halo effect that exists for the skilled fe-ale business golfer. Not only is golf a great equalizer, but people tend to generalize and believe that if a woman is competent in golf, she must also be competent in business. This halo effect seems to work for women in a way that it does not for men. And it works with employers and clients alike.

Debra Brumitt, founder of *Golf for Women* magazine, says women often tell her that if they are competent at golf, the boss looks at them differently and they are perceived as having more in common back in the office. Another female senior-level executive pointed out just how strong this golf bond can be when she told of running into a former client who had been retired for about five years. The first thing he said was, "How's your golf game?" Of the hundreds of conversations they had had, it was golf that made them kindred spirits.

This powerful aspect of business golf can really give a woman the competitive edge that will then allow her to use all her other business skills to best advantage. As women have learned in business, they have to play the game as women, not as male clones.

Special Tips for Women

Here are some additional helpful hints women who play business golf should be aware of.

1. **Be proficient.** You can play business golf effectively even if your skill level isn't the greatest, but there seems to be a higher correlation for women than for men between high golf skill and great success in business golf.
    *   Take lessons and practice to improve your skills, just as you would any other business skill. The payoffs can be great.
    *   Focus on your short game - chipping and putting. With some practice, women tend to excel at putting. It is much more difficult for the average women to get the distance. So it is easier to trim your score by working on your short game.
    *   Make sure you know the rules and etiquette. Always keep the number one rule in mind - keep up the pace.
    *   If you are really good, don't hold back unless you sense you really need to. You will find some men are threatened by your skill level, but most will appreciate it and hold you in higher esteem. Play customer golf only if you believe it is best for business.
2. **Don't try to be one of the boys.** Swearing, losing your temper, and drinking too much are taboo for all business golfers, but especially so for women. Just as a high skill level has a halo effect, this behavior has a horns effect, where the negative perception created by the behavior is generalized. Just as the halo effect is stronger for women than for men, so is the horns effect. Don't degrade yourself and hurt your business opportunities by trying to be one of the boys, even if they are leading the way.
3. **Advance the cause of business golf for women.**
    *   Keep a log of all business resulting from golf. Once management sees how you are impacting the bottom line using business golf, they'll be more apt to support your efforts by giving you more time to play, including you in outings and paying for them, and working on getting the rules changed at restricted clubs.
    *   Find a mentor within the company whom you can play with. This will not only help your career, but can change the perception of the value of business golf for women.
    *   Support female pros. Take lessons with a female teaching pro. Female pros are better prepared to understand the unique challenges facing women in golf. And they often have better teaching skills, since many of them have degrees in education, which most of the male pros do not.
    *   If your spouse is a member of a club that discriminates in any way, become involved in club committees and work to get the

by-laws changed. Women have successfully done this at several clubs in the New York-metropolitan area.

- Get involved in the Executive Women's Golf League. This will benefit you on a personal level and may also help to end the discrimination against women in golf.

Summary

Although it may be more difficult for women to use golf as a business tool, it is definitely worth the effort because the value of business golf can be greater for women than for men. The double standards, negative attitudes, and gender bias that exist elsewhere also exist in golf. It is important for everyone to be aware of these issues and to strategically fight for equality in golf. Then it is very possible that the glass ceiling will indeed be broken by a golf ball.

The Worlds Greatest Water Hazards
International Business Golf

I read some interesting statistics recently that provide real insight into the concept of a global economy. If the world were a town of 1,000 people, 564 of the citizens would be Asians, 210 Europeans, 86 Africans, 80 South American, and only 60 would be North Americans. Unfortunately, the statistic wasn't broken down into how many of the 60 North Americans were from Mexico and Canada. But it does make it clear that although the U.S. holds a prominent position in world affairs, we are clearly in the minority in terms of sheer numbers.

Another statistic quoted Alan Greenspan, chairman of the Federal Reserve, as saying that since 1980, foreign investments in the U.S. have increased by 300 percent. These statistics validate what we already know is true. More and more, we are doing business with people from other countries. And the majority of these people are from countries whose culture is very different than ours.

Despite the differences, there is one thing we have in common with countries around the world - the love of golf. Golf is a universal game. So when you are involved in international business, it is just a matter of time before you'll find yourself on the golf course with someone from another country and another culture. Then, in addition to knowing the golf etiquette and the business etiquette, you'll also want to know as much as possible about that culture and how they do business. Otherwise, your drive won't make it across the Atlantic or Pacific. You'll end up in the water hazard known as the gulf of misunderstanding between people - and it could cost you business.

Cultures Have Basic Behavioral Styles

In Chapter 11, we looked at certain behavioral characteristics an individual might have based on family influences, environment, life experiences, and *cultural influences.* Just as the culture helps shape individuals, the behavioral patterns of the individuals are often reflected in the culture. So countries and cultures can also have a *perceived* behavioral style. Knowledge of these can be helpful in understanding people, as long as we are careful not to overgeneralize or stereotype people. Remember the points made in Chapter 11 about individual behaviors. Use what you know about a country's perceived style as a tool, but don't pigeonhole people.

It's important to remember that we're dealing with behavioral tendencies: The culture's values, beliefs, and traditions will influence its citizens' behavior, but individuals are still unique and can choose a variety of behaviors. Also, the global economy and mass communication have allowed us to experience and assimilate aspects of many countries and cultures. Still, when we're relating to someone from another country or culture, it's helpful to start with our general perceptions.

Think of Italy, for example. You probably think of people who enjoy other people and are outgoing and warm. They like to entertain and enjoy the attention of others. When you think of Italians, you very often think of Socializers. Now think of Germany. You probably came up with a picture of a Director - someone who is results-oriented, tries hard to be the best, makes decisions easily, and is focused on the task.

In the same way, think of Spain. The characteristics of Relaters probably come to mind: easygoing, patient, persistent, slower paced. In contrast, Japan brings to mind the Thinker pattern: slow-paced, concerned with details, perfectionists, very observant of what is happening around them.

To learn as much as possible about your international associates, begin with what you perceive and observe about their culture's or country's behavioral pattern. Always beware of stereotypes. Use your know-ledge of cultural and national behavioral styles, along with any other information you have, as a tool to help you decide how to adapt your behavior with a particular individual in a particular situation.

Think in terms of how business is conducted and how relationships are built in the person's homeland. Take the time to research this if you don't feel comfortable with your level of understanding about possible cultural differences. Get some pointers from people you know who have experience playing golf with business associates from other countries.

Then pay special attention to how Westernized the person is - how much time they've spent here, how often they've played golf in this country, and how similar their country's life-style and values are to those here. Then adapt your behavioral style accordingly. For example, you'd probably find fewer cultural differences playing with an European national than you would with a Japanese national. Likewise, a Japanese national who has relocated here for business may have adapted to the Western culture. Therefore, you wouldn't need to adapt your style as much as you would for a first-time visitor from Japan.

An International Golf Strategy Model

When I asked business golfers about their experiences with players from other countries, they most often began talking about the Japanese. They explained it was because the cultural differences are greater between East and West than between European counties and the United States. Also, the Japanese are often much more interested in playing golf than business associates from other countries. For these reasons, the rest of this chapter will focus on some of the things you need to know to adapt your style when playing with someone from Japan. If you are playing with someone from another country, use this as a model to decide what might be a consideration in modifying your style.

Playing With Japanese Business Associates

Japan seems to have fallen in love with golf. Because of limited available land, however, there are very few golf courses. Club memberships are limited and extremely expensive. Multi-level driving ranges are popular even though a bucket of balls can cost more than $20 on the highest (cheapest) deck. Golf pros have told me that it is not uncommon for Japanese who sign up for lessons to have great skill because of their driving range experience - even though they've never been out on a course!

This love of golf provides a perfect opportunity to entertain Japanese associates. Golf can be a good icebreaker and a great way to find a common ground. To ensure a successful round, you'll want to keep these basic Japanese characteristics in mind.

- Relationships are extremely important and carry greater weight than the business at hand. Social activities are used to strengthen business ties. Follow up is important and signifies the on-going nature of the relationship.
- Harmony in relationships is critical and must be maintained at all cost. Unlike Americans, who can "agree to disagree," the Japanese view differences as damaging to the relationship. The ability to compromise is valued.
- Trust is critical to a business relationship. The Japanese want to know the kind of person you are before deciding to do business.

Several meetings usually take place before business is discussed at all.

- Proper etiquette and form are very important. The Japanese tend to be much more formal than Americans.
- The rules are very important. The Japanese are less likely to defy authority than Americans are.
- Being quiet and a good listener are valued. Stating your opinions too quickly can be perceived as an inability or unwillingness to think things through or to consider all the details.
- Business decisions are often made by consensus. You may find you are dealing with several Japanese executives at once, both on and off the course.
- The Japanese are concerned with the process and don't like to be rushed. Plan to spend much more time developing the relationship and doing business than you normally might.

In addition to these general considerations, the people I interviewed also shared various tips on planning your business golf strategy for a round with a Japanese associate.

Developing an Appropriate Business Golf Strategy

Have a pre-round meeting to brief work team members who are part of the foursome about cultural differences. Develop a specific strategy that everyone agrees to use. Because in Japan management by consensus is often the rule, you'll want to make sure everyone is on the same wavelength and presents a united front.

Learn as much about Japanese customs and history as you can. Get as many details as possible about the associate's background and the company history. Plan to use this information in the conversation. It will show your concern and help develop the relationship. Using Japanese customs such as bowing will help you make a favorable impression.

Find out how frequently your guests play on American courses. Do everything you can to make them feel comfortable during the round. Don't assume they know how to drive a golf cart.

Develop an opening statement to welcome your guest in a formal way. The senior person from your team should initially act as spokesperson and address the senior Japanese executive, even if a junior-level person has been your contact.

Also check your approach to the game. Review the rules. They are very important to the Japanese. Remember that golf is a very revealing game and the Japanese are very observant. If you tend to have a problem with your temper on the golf course, focus on how you can control your feelings. Self-control is very important to the Japanese.

Be prepared to keep up the pace without it appearing rushed. Above all, focus on enjoying every aspect of the round. The Japanese are very much into the total experience of golf as well as the game itself.

When getting started:

- Arrive on time. A late arrival is considered an insult.
- If you are not sure of the pronunciation of a name, ask. It will show you care and respect the person.
- Business cards are essential to the Japanese and considered an extension of the person. When you ask for the business card, read it very carefully and acknowledge the person as you are reading it. Treat the card with respect. Don't write on it or casually shove it in your pocket. Put it away carefully in a safe place.
- Formally introduce everyone present. Knowing everyone's status is very important to the Japanese, as well.
- Avoid using first names unless the Japanese invite you to do so.

The giving of gifts can take on greater significance when you are in a business relationship with the Japanese. Many golfers have told me it is not uncommon that you will be presented with a gift when you have invited someone from Japan to play. Presenting your guest with a gift is a great way to communicate respect and build the relationship. However, keep these points in mind.

- Unless you have something for everyone, give the gift when you are alone.
- Make sure the gift is wrapped. An elaborate package or a fancy container are just as important as the gift itself. An unwrapped gift communicates that the person is not important enough for you to bother.
- The appropriateness of the gift and care you take in selecting it are much more important than the value of the gift. Try to think of something that the person would really enjoy that might not normally be available to them. Golf-related items, gourmet foods, and small gifts with regional significance are usually appreciated.
- Remember the gift is a token and should not outdo any gift you may receive from them.
- In Japan, a gift is given with both hands. Doing so will communicate respect and also your understanding of Japanese customs.
- A nicely framed photo taken during the round is a great follow-up gift, especially if the person is also into photography.

- When you are presented with a gift, it is considered polite to refuse it once or twice before you finally accept it. The next time you see the person, it is considered good etiquette to mention the gift and how much you enjoyed it.

When you develop your conversation strategy, keep cultural differences in mind. This is important because the appropriateness of topics and the way messages are delivered and received vary from culture to culture.

Here are some tips for selecting topics when you are playing with someone from Japan:

- Avoid controversial topics or anything that could lead to debate.
- Don't ask personal questions.
- Safe topics that are generally of interest to the Japanese are sports (golf and baseball are typical favorites), travel, history, and often photography.
- Talk about your favorable impressions of Japan - paintings, history, culture, etc.
- Don't praise yourself. Modesty is a virtue.
- Don't criticize your competition - or anyone else. Remember, compromise is highly valued.
- Don't joke too much. Adults are expected to be serious minded.
- Be careful with compliments. Too much praise can make the Japanese uncomfortable and may be perceived as insincere. Indirect compliments often work best. For example, instead of, "That was an incredible shot. You really have a strong drive," you might say something like, "Great skill is required to keep the ball out of the woods on this hole."

When delivering your message:

- Don't speak too loudly.
- Don't say "no," which is considered rude. If you say something like "It is very difficult." or "I'll think about it." instead, you'll maintain the harmony of the relationship.
- Don't respond too quickly. Pause while you think about what has just been said. Use silence to communicate that you are contemplating a message that has importance.
- Many Japanese are more familiar with written English than spoken English. They may have difficulty understanding you but will not say so because it is considered impolite. Make your message as clear as you possibly can.

- Be very aware of your nonverbal message and keep it rather formal:
  1. Japanese require more personal space than Westerners. Don't get too close. A safe bet is to double the distance that would be appropriate with an American colleague.
  2. Don't touch. It is considered an invasion of privacy.
  3. Japanese gestures tend to be more subdued than those of many Americans. Tone down your gestures, if necessary, so you are perceived as a serious, responsible person.
  4. Dress conservatively and avoid clothing or accessories that may be considered flashy or inappropriate. Women may want to avoid wearing slacks, a lot of jewelry, or heavy perfume.

When listening to and understanding the Japanese:

- Listen between the lines. The Japanese tend to express their ideas and feelings in an indirect way.
- Nodding means the Japanese understand, not that they agree.
- Often when the Japanese ask for an opinion, they are looking for reassurance rather than honest feedback. Be sensitive to their feelings and don't be critical.
- The Japanese may respond with what they think you want to hear because politeness and keeping harmony are so important.
- If a message is interpreted, look at the speaker, not at the interpreter.

Because social activities in Japan are an important part of business and are used to strengthen the business relationship, the 19th hole will take on special significance. As with the round itself, let your Japanese guest set the pace and the level of formality.

Once the relationship is solidified and trust has been established, you may find that the Japanese tend to relax quite a bit during the 19th hole. In Japan, drinking with business associates is a way to settle issues from the workplace in a non-threatening way. The following day, no one talks about what was discussed because it was outside the realm of work and mentioned while drinking. However, based on what was discussed, the participants may make work-related changes to improve the business relationship. It is a subtle way to deal with issues without anyone losing face. Wait for your Japanese associate to bring up business. If it happens, you'll have a sure sign that the relationship is on solid ground.

Although business may be discussed over drinks, it probably won't be brought up during a meal. Just as the Japanese respect and enjoy the game of golf on several levels, they also approach eating in the same way. Business discussions are considered inappropriate. It is also impolite to say you are hungry, eat too quickly, or take very large portions. Focus on the enjoyment of the meal and follow the lead set by your guest.

As important as it is in any business relationship, follow up is even more critical when dealing with the Japanese. Lack of follow up can severely damage the relationship because it communicates your lack of concern. So after the round of golf, you'll want to thank your associate for an enjoyable day, mention how much you value any gift you received, and set a date for a future meeting or phone call. Again, taking a photo of the foursome is a great way to ensure you'll be in touch soon.

Summary:

In a global economy, the chances are good that you'll eventually play golf with a business associate from another country. You'll want to learn as much as possible about their culture beforehand so you don't accidentally damage the relationship.

This chapter focuses on the types of things you might want to know before playing with someone from Japan. Japan was selected because the Japanese play such an important role in international business, are so in love with golf, and are from a culture that most Westerners don't understand very well. If you are playing with someone from a different country, use this chapter as a model, to help you think of the kind of information you'll want to be familiar with before the round. You may find someone in your company or at your favorite course who has a wealth of information about playing with visitors from other countries.

However you gather the information, remember that you are dealing with individuals. Don't stereotype or pre-judge. If you are in doubt or feel uncomfortable because of cultural differences or a language barrier, remember that golf, an appreciation for good manners, smiling, and having fun are all universal!

Playing a Round on the Square
The Ethical Considerations in Business Golf

Bobby Jones lost the U.S. Open in 1925. His ball was in the woods and it moved when he addressed it. Although no one saw this, Jones called a penalty on himself, which ultimately cost him the tournament. The media focused on what they perceived as a remarkable gesture of good sportsmanship. Jones passed it off by saying, "You might as well praise a man for not robbing a bank as to praise him for playing by the rules." This is just one example of the great respect golfers have for the game.

Throughout its history, golf has always been associated with good manners, integrity, honor, and honesty. Golfers are aware of this and tend to very seriously live up to this tradition. Professional players have reflected this high standard and stories abound about golfers choosing to do the right thing even if it is in conflict with their best personal interests.

Ironically, there are just as many stories, quips, and jokes about cheating at golf. Play the game and face its many challenges and frustrations and you'll understand why someone once said that nothing handicaps you so much in golf as honesty! It is not always easy to "play the ball as it lies and the course as you find it." Yet this is what the honorable game of golf demands. This creates a moral dilemma that eventually most golfers have to face, whether they are playing recreational golf or business golf.

When you play business golf, the ethical and moral considerations are greater and the stakes are higher. It is important to be aware of these issues and to think them through before you are confronted by them. A little values clarification up front could save you a tough business decision down the line and could even save you an important client. So as you read about these social and ethical issues, think about how you would handle the situation if it came up.

Discrimination

In Chapter 13 we looked at the discrimination that exists against women in golf: restricted tee times, limited access to club membership and facilities, and the failure of management to accept the value of golf as a business tool for women. If you are a woman, expect to run into discrimination in golf. It still exists in society in general, so why should golf be any different?

Think about how you can best handle it. You'll want to develop a strategy that will promote your rights and fight the discrimination and at the same time also protect and advance your business opportunities. Chapter 13 provides specifics recommendations that can help you do this (develop your golf skill, keep a business golf log, join the Executive Women's Golf League).

Also think about what you would do or say as a target of gender bias. If you were the judge who was denied access to the Men's Grill, how would you handle it? Would you deal with it differently if it were a social rather than a business situation?

If you are a man, it is just as important to be aware of these issues and to examine your true feelings and attitudes regarding women business golfers. Would you invite a female business associate for a round of golf as readily as you would a male associate? Would your behavior be different if you were playing with a man? How would you handle the situation if you were hosting an important female client and your club had discriminatory restrictions? If you are in a management position, are you providing equal opportunities for female as well as male employees to use business golf? How comfortable are you in accepting an invitation to play from a female business associate? As more and more women advance in professional and management positions, more and more men will have to face these issues.

It is helpful to know up front how you'll handle them so when they come up, you won't endanger the business relationship by behaving inappropriately.

Another area of discrimination in golf involves minority groups. Although the PGA as well as other golf organizations have taken steps to end discrimination against minorities, unfortunately it still exists. As the glass ceiling is broken by more and more members of minority groups, it is important to check your values and attitudes regarding this type of discrimination, if you haven't already done so. For example, what would you do if your company held a corporate membership at a restricted country club and you wanted to entertain a minority client there? When you golf with someone of a different race or culture, what are your expectations and your biases? If you haven't dealt with this issue yet, it is important to give it some thought. Awareness is the first step toward dealing with it in a morally correct and business enhancing way.

To a lesser degree, discrimination of new golfers by veteran golfers also exists. It grows out of the perception that new golfers crowd the course, slow down the game, are not serious golfers, and don't respect the game or the course. It is so strong that the National Golf Foundation has identified it as a major concern and is working with its member courses to increase awareness and to end it. The key is education - getting the veteran golfers to empathize, help out, and have more patience, and getting the newer players to learn the game and take it seriously.

If you are a business golfer who has been playing for a while, check your attitude toward new golfers. Think back to when you first played and work to turn any annoyance and resentment you may feel into a willingness to help newcomers learn the game and love the game as much as you do.

If you are a new golfer, *learn the game*! Your skill level doesn't have to be great, just don't slow down play. Know the rules, know the etiquette, and show that you are a serious student of the game. Be open to suggestions from seasoned players. Don't let your behavior be a good cause for anyone to get annoyed.

Knowledge of the rules and empathy to the needs of other golfers can overcome this type of discrimination if it is a reaction to newcomers' behavior. It is more difficult to deal with when the veteran golfers are entrenched in the old-boy mentality and discriminate because they perceive that new golfers are invading their domain.

Whatever form it takes, discrimination is a very real issue in golf. It is important to think about it in terms of your values and attitudes and know where you stand before the issues come up, because in business golf, your discrimination not only labels you as a bigot, it could also cost you business.

Beyond discrimination, which exists in both recreational and business golf, there are several other ethical considerations that are specific to business golf. Some of the executives I interviewed expressed real concern over them; others viewed it as just a part of business golf and no big deal. However you reconcile these issues with your own personal value system, it is important to be aware that they do exist and to know that they can significantly impact a business relationship.

The Hidden Cost of Business Golf

Whether it is client entertainment or employee development, business golf costs money. Sometimes a *lot of money*. Who actually picks up the tab? The customer. Of course, we all know you have to spend money to make money, and if it wasn't business golf, it would be some other form of client entertainment, employee incentive, or team-building activity.

But when does this valuable business tool become a lavish perk that has more to do with personal gratification than business? How much should be spent on business golf, and how do you measure the cost effectiveness of it? Is there another, less expensive way to achieve the same results? These are some of the questions the decision makers in corporate America need to ask. This really becomes an ethical consideration in times of rightsizing and massive layoffs, when the high cost of business golf may be reflected not only in higher shelf prices but also in higher unemployment rates.

I certainly am not suggesting a "down with business golf" movement. I firmly believe that golf is a valuable business tool that can give you a competitive edge. I'm simply suggesting that we look carefully at how we use business golf so we don't slip back into the "greed is good" excesses of the eighties.

As a business tool, golf is very much like advertising. The cost can be high and the effectiveness can be difficult to measure. As someone once said, half the money spent on advertising is wasted, but it is impossible to tell which half. The same may be true of business golf. Still, it is possible with both tools to look at how the money is spent and to make a decision about how the tool is used and its cost-effectiveness. With golf, it may be more difficult to do because people love to play, so the ego investment is higher. This is true, whether the form of business golf a company uses is a single round in a foursome, VIP golf, or "ultimate golf experiences." But the ethical considerations are often greater with VIP golf and ultimate golf experiences because of the higher costs involved.

VIP Golf

Most people enjoy meeting someone famous- and business has used this to its advantage for many years. Authors draw crowds at book signings, soap opera stars appear at malls and attract hoards of adoring fans, and sports and show business personalities can increase product sales with an autograph-signing session. Business booms because the customer has very brief contact with someone famous - and feels special because of it. VIP golf is a variation of this and is much more powerful because it provides a more intense, personalized experience that really is an esteem builder for the client or employee.

There are several types of VIP golf but they all involve celebrities who are paid to participate in a business golf event. The celebrities are usually golf pros, although it is becoming more popular to include football, basketball, and show business stars in these business golf activities.

The VIP's responsibilities may include playing a round of golf with clients or employees and mixing and mingling at cocktail parties and other social functions. The golf VIPs may also be asked to present a skills clinic or give a speech.

The concept of VIP golf is not new. It goes back at least to the turn of the century when Harry Vardon, who won six British Opens and a U.S. Open and is credited with developing the Vardon grip, demonstrated his golf skills for the customers of the Jordan Marsh department store.

Today it is not unusual for a golf VIP to receive $25,000 or more to attend a one-day business conference that might include a round of golf or a skills clinic and an after-dinner speech.

It is not just large corporations that use VIP golf as a business tool. Many smaller companies and non-profit organizations that sponsor outings use well-known local pros to increase the popularity of an event. The cost may be as little as $1,000, but the perceived value for these organizations is much greater.

The setting for VIP golf varies, from a meeting at corporate headquarters to a regional conference to a pro am event to an international tour. Some of these events are outings. Others are better described as ultimate golf experiences.

Ultimate Golf Experiences

An ultimate golf experience is any event that is a golfer's dream come true: that makes you the envy of all your friends; that is almost impossible to do on your own regardless of money or status; and that you'll be talking about forever and ever. That's what it means to the invited client or employee (and their lucky guest). To the company sponsoring the event, it means megabucks. The hope is that the fortune spent will generate multi-megabucks in additional business.

The scope of ultimate golf experiences is international, and destinations in Scotland, England, and Portugal are very popular. For example, a company in the hospitality industry hosted a two-week excursion that included golf at St. Andrews in Scotland as well as several days at the Ryder Cup competition. That is certainly a golfer's dream come true - especially when someone else is picking up the tab! In this case, the cost is no doubt passed along to the consumer and reflected in the price of the product.

In terms of values clarification about the cost of business golf, it is important to know how business golf can be used - and misused. Your personal value system will help you determine the line between use and abuse. Your good business sense will help you decide if the results justify your expenditures on business golf. And your common sense will tell you that the more lavishly you entertain clients and employees today, the greater their expectations will be when you entertain them a few months from now. This can very easily lead to a "can you top this?" mentality that may not be cost-effective.

One way you can decide how you can use business golf most effectively is to look at the cost-benefit ratio discussed earlier. If you determine that the maximum amount of business you might get from a prospect or client is "X" amount of dollars, then you can decide how much you are willing to spend to get that amount of business. For some clients, an occasional round of golf would do it. For larger accounts, a weekend excursion or invitation to a pro-am may be appropriate. For a handful of very big clients, an ultimate golf experience might even be justified. When you use cost-effectiveness as the basis for your decision, some prospects, clients, and employees just won't make the cut to be included in the more lavish business golf events.

But cost-effectiveness may not be the only consideration. In client entertainment, the rule of reciprocity also comes into play.

Client Entertainment

Whether you are the host or the guest, when business golf is used for client or prospect entertainment, the rule of reciprocity and gift giving become real ethical concerns. Although this occurs more in certain industries, it is important for all business golfers to be aware of the issues.

The Rule of Reciprocity

The old saying "one hand washes the other" is pretty much the basis for the rule of reciprocity. In a relationship of equals, if you do something nice for me, it is expected that I'll do something nice for you. If you do something *extremely* nice for me (like inviting me for an ultimate golf experience) and I can't do something equally nice for you (say, giving you a million dollars worth of business), then the relationship becomes unbalanced. The rule of reciprocity states that a tacit "IOU" is set up to bring the relationship back into balance and that somewhere down the line, I am expected to reciprocate in order to keep the relationship on an even keel. Ethical considerations and moral dilemmas can grow out of the rule of reciprocity.

To look at the ethical considerations, you have to look at the basic reciprocity agreement that business is based on. You are providing a quality product or service in exchange for a fair price. Business golf can be viewed as a "value-added" by your client. When does the value-added tip the scale so far out of balance that it becomes a question of ethics? What kind of tacit IOUs are you comfortable setting up and how is the client going to deal with paying them back?

Viewing it from the client's perspective helps you focus on any ethical concerns. So pretend you are the client. Then revise the dollar amounts of your expectations and reduce the lavishness of the business golf event if you feel it is required. And be sure to include the cost of any gifts that may be part of the business golf event.

Gift Giving

When a non-profit organization sponsors a golf outing, gift giving is typically a part of it. Local companies will donate prizes and usually each participant will receive a package of promotional give-away items, such as tote bags, golf hats, or golf balls.

Gift giving is also very common when corporations use golf outings for client or employee entertainment. The difference is that when a participant pays a registration fee for an outing, the reciprocity agreement is never out of balance. No matter how valuable the prizes, nothing beyond the registration fee is expected from the participant. When business gets into gift giving, the reciprocity agreement can be affected, depending on the value of the gift. In some cases it can also create a real dilemma if the recipient is bound by a code of conduct.

For some executives, especially within the financial industry, receiving expensive gifts is tantamount to accepting a bribe. Employees may even sign a code of conduct that precludes their accepting gifts over a certain value. This is also often the case with companies who put contracts out to bid. Be sensitive to the possibility that your gift giving may create a moral dilemma for the recipient.

An executive at a nationally known insurance company that regularly uses golf outings for client entertainment told me about a client who tried to balance the reciprocity agreement by presenting him with a set of golf clubs. The estimated value of the clubs and bag was several thousand dollars! To accept the gift would have been a violation of the code of conduct and could have jeopardized his job. To refuse it could have resulted in losing a big account, since the client was from Japan, where refusing a gift is considered a breach of etiquette. What would you do in this tough situation? Fortunately, the executive has able to graciously refuse the clubs by explaining his morale dilemma.

Obviously, the best thing to do is to avoid getting into the situation in the first place. Don't try to buy business with overly extravagant entertaining and gift giving. And be sensitive to the situation the entertaining and gift giving creates for the other person.

Customer Golf

If you play well, there is another ethical consideration that may come up when you use golf for client entertainment. Should you let the client win? If you do, you are into playing what is generally known as "customer golf."

How will you deal with it if the only way to achieve a good business relationship is to let the customer or boss win? If you are not a great golfer, you may never have to deal with this issue. If you play well and are very competitive about the game, it may or may not be an ethical concern for you. But at least be aware it exists or it can take you by surprise, as it did a few people I talked to.

One executive told me that before a company golf outing, everyone was told to let the president win. I also was told about a company president who used a tee for every shot, except when on the green. New employees were briefed not to mention that this was against the rules. As someone once said, show me a good loser and I'll show you someone who is playing golf with the boss! How would *you* feel about "letting someone win," rather than playing your best?

If this is an ethical issue for you, define your focus and it will probably be less of a problem. Several executives told me that when they define the game as business golf and focus on providing the best time for the client or boss, they automatically play less competitively.

A story about the golf great Byron Nelson also illustrates the concept. Before Nelson played a course, he would always discreetly find out who held the course record. If it was a local pro or amateur, he wouldn't try to break the record because he knew it meant more to the other person than it did to him. It is a matter of what goal you focus on. If winning is important to the client or boss, don't focus on winning at golf. Focus on winning at business!

Cheating

But what if the only way someone can win is by cheating? How would you handle that? Most golfers hate people who cheat at golf. The Hyatt Study came up with some pretty interesting statistics on cheating. More than 80 percent of the executives surveyed agreed that they hated people who cheat at golf. Most (87 percent) said they had played with someone who'd cheated. About half said they had confronted the person who cheated, with almost a third saying they were more likely to confront the person in front of others. How embarrassing for the person who was cheating! But since they have to catch you to hate you and embarrass you, a lot of people do cheat.

Over half (55 percent) of the Hyatt respondents admitted to cheating at least once. This most often involved moving the ball to a better lie, but also included not counting shots and taking Mulligans without approval.

As a business golfer, it is important to be clear in your values about cheating. Would you confront a business associate who cheated or would you let it fall under the heading of customer golf? Would you cheat if you thought no one would know? And how can you be sure no one will know?

A story I heard points out that honesty really is the best policy. Two men were fishing just off shore on Long Island's Great South Bay where one of the greens of a private course abuts the water. As they waited for a bite, the fishermen watched several foursomes play the hole. Suddenly a ball overshot the green and landed in the sand at water's edge. A man soon approached the green, looked around, optimistically checked the cup, and finally discovered the ball on the sandy shore. He looked back to see if the others in the foursome could see him and then picked up the ball and tossed it on the green!

Little did he know that the fishermen were in the 83 percent who hate cheaters. They started waving their arms to get his attention and yelling that they had seen what he did.

Now imagine that you are that golfer and you are out with an important client and your boss. What would you do? You probably don't have enough time to place the ball back in the sand, or do you? How could you explain it if the boss sees you? Maybe it is best to leave it. But what if the fishermen start signaling to the rest of your foursome, and your boss and client find out you've cheated?

Suppose you are the boss or the client and you caught the cheater in the act. How would you handle it? How would your feelings about him change in terms of wanting to do business with him?

A golfer in an old joke says it's not that he cheats, it's just that he plays for his health and a low score makes him feel better. In business golf, cheating creates too much stress and anxiety to be good for your health. And it is definitely not good for business!

Gambling

What may be good for business but may be an ethical concern for some is the common practice of gambling during a round of golf. Wagering is so much a part of golf that Chapter 17 goes into detail on the topic. Most of the executives I interviewed said that they usually set up some sort of side game to keep the round interesting. The Hyatt Study backed this up, with over two-thirds of the respondents saying they had gambled, many on a regular basis.

Perhaps gambling is so popular because it makes the game more competitive. Since people in business tend to thrive on competition, gambling in business golf is very prevalent. If this creates a moral or ethical dilemma for you, be prepared to deal with the issue. It *is* possible to maintain your values without damaging the business relationship.

Summary

When you use golf as a business tool, it is important to be aware of the various ethical considerations and to reconcile the issues with your own personal value system before they arise. Know where you stand and how you would handle discrimination and cheating on the golf course. Decide how you feel about gambling and playing customer golf. Be aware of the distinctions between use and abuse in business golf and define your own limits in terms of VIP golf, client entertainment, and gift giving.

Once you know where you stand on these issues, you can develop a tentative action plan for dealing with them that will be consistent with your values.

When Tee Time Isn't Your Cup of Tea
How to Use Business Golf Even If You Don't Play

Now suppose you don't agree with Chi Chi Rodriguez who said that, "Golf is the most fun you can have without taking your clothes off." You believe that the best thing about golf is that it isn't compulsory. And you cheer the sportswriter Westbrook Pegler for saying, "Golf is the most useless outdoor game ever devised to waste and try the spirit of man [woman, too!]." You even agree with President Richard M. Nixon's view that, "By the time you get dressed, drive out there, play 18 holes, and come home, you've blown seven hours. There are better things you can do with your time."

I respect your opinion. Golf isn't for everyone. But since it can be a useful business tool, you'll at least want to explore the possibilities. And who knows. You may even get to like it. A lot of avid golfers once thought it was a waste of time - until they played a few rounds and got hooked!

So if you've never played, try it. If you've tried it and didn't like it, be open-minded and give it a second chance. And even if you discover you don't like it or, worse yet, really hate it, you can still benefit from the many business golf opportunities available.

Try It Without Making a Major Commitment

Golf as a business skill can be as valuable as computer expertise. Not everyone initially feels at ease with a computer. Nor is everyone destined to become a computer whiz. But most people in business recognize the importance of being computer literate. Likewise, even if you don't enjoy golf enough to become a serious recreational golfer, you'll still want to become golf literate because it is a business tool that can give you a definite advantage.

Be Willing to Learn

Before you head for the golf course or driving range, learn the basics of the game from an expert. Sign up for a low-cost adult education class or take at least one lesson from a club pro. If nothing else, rent a video from the library so you understand the principles of grip, aim, and setup. Also read books or magazines to become really familiar with the game. Then make a limited commitment to yourself to practice the skills. This is the only way to find out if you like the game or not.

The Learning Is in the Doing

Work on your putting skills first to help build your confidence. Practice greens at public courses are free. Playing a round of miniature golf is also a fun way to practice putting without investing a lot of time or money.

Once you feel comfortable putting, try the driving range. After a few sessions there, put it all together by playing a round at a par 3 or pitch and putt course. Follow this up with nine holes at a regulation course. Now you are ready to play a full round of eighteen holes. Be sure to select a course that is recommended for beginners.

This process is sort of like the desensitization used to help people overcome phobias. It will help you get acquainted with golf without feeling overwhelmed or frustrated. And you'll build your skills and confidence by learning in manageable increments.

Even if you come to the conclusion that golf is not for you, at least you will be golf literate and prepared to use business golf if necessary.

How to Use It Even if You Don't Like It

If you have tried golf and you don't like it, what this really means is you'll probably never become a *recreational* golfer. Many golfers out there are saying, "Great! The courses are crowded enough already!"

Don't try to force yourself to like it. You won't be happy and the others in your foursome probably won't be either. But before writing golf off completely, take a look at what business golf can do for you. Because even if you are not a recreational golfer, you can still be a business golfer!

Weigh the advantages of using business golf against how you feel about the game. Think about how your profession, industry, and organization use business golf and how you might use it to reach your career goals. Perhaps you are in a field where business golf isn't used extensively. You can use other sport or social functions to provide the same advantages as business golf. You don't stand to lose anything by avoiding business golf.

But what if business golf is popular in your organization and your industry and you realize you are at a disadvantage if you don't play. Then what? Find other ways to achieve the same results. Join civic organizations to network, use business lunches or dinners to entertain clients, and office parties to develop rapport with senior management. But when absolutely necessary, use business golf.

When 'Ya Gotta'

So you'd rather have a root canal than play business golf. But golf is the only way to connect with a certain client or really get the ear of the CEO. If this is the case, think of it the way you would a business cocktail party you don't want to attend: Make the best of it, work it to your advantage, and enjoy it on whatever level you can.

Be in the know and ready to go. You gave golf a fair chance by taking a few lessons and reading a few books. So you know the appropriate dress and the ins and outs of golf etiquette. You have the basic equipment and understand the principles (even if you don't have a high skill level). You are set to play an occasional round of business golf without embarrassing yourself. To maintain and develop your level of competence, you'll want to practice occasionally on the putting green or driving range.

Arrange an appropriate activity. If you are not a serious golfer, select a form of business golf that your business associates will enjoy and that is comfortable for you. Outings with a Scramble format are fun and popular for golfers at any level. If playing in a foursome, choose a course that is not too challenging. When formats or side action are discussed before the round, suggest a round-robin or something like Bingo Bango Bongo that keeps everyone in the game. (See Chapter 17 for an explanation of various formats.) Remember that one of the objectives of your business golf agenda is to make sure everyone is having a good time - including you.

Enjoy it! Look closely enough and you'll discover *something* you can enjoy during the round even if you are not into golf. The beautiful setting, the social interaction, the 19th hole lunch, and the business opportunities can make it a positive and valuable experience for you. Screen for the positive, relax, and enjoy yourself.

Remember, for you golf is just a game, so don't take it too seriously. Also remember that business golf is a valuable tool that you can use effectively even if you don't like the game. So make the best of it, regardless of how you feel.

How to Use It Even if You Hate It

Hard to imagine, but there are some people who never, ever want to play a round of golf. They just don't like the game or maybe aren't willing to make the time investment necessary to bring their skills up to a respectable level. If they are in an industry or profession that doesn't use business golf extensively, no problem. But if that is not the case, they can still use business golf effectively and gain many of the advantages - without ever playing at all.

If the last paragraph pretty much sums up how *you* feel about golf, you've probably already found alternatives to business golf that provide opportunities to network and entertain clients. But since you'll also be using business golf, even if on a limited, non-participating basis, you'll still need to be golf literate. That is why it is important to go through the step of trying it before you make the decision it's not for you.

There are several ways you can use golf as an effective business tool even if you don't play. Most of them involve golf as a spectator sport.

Follow the pros so you feel comfortable talking about golf. This involves a very minimal time commitment. Read the sports section or watch the sports news on TV to learn what PGA (LPGA and Senior PGA, too) events are coming up and where they will be held. If it is a major event, watch as much of it on TV as you can. At the very least, listen to the Sunday evening sports news so you'll know who won and if there were any really exciting moments (hole-in-one, playoffs, etcetera).

Do this long enough and you'll become quite knowledgeable. And you'll soon reach a comfort level at which you'll feel confident initiating a golf conversation with a business associate you know is into golf - a good way to build rapport! When they ask if you play, you can say you're into tennis (or whatever your thing is) but enjoy following the pros. They'll respect you for caring enough to talk about something they love.

Keep up on golf as you would any current event. It can help build or advance business relationships. If nothing else, when someone mentions Jack Nicklaus, you won't embarrass yourself by saying you've been a fan ever since you saw him in *Easy Rider*! You may even get hooked on golf as a spectator sport, which can provide many more business opportunities.

If you don't enjoy playing, you can use golf as a spectator sport. Depending on the type of event and your level of involvement, you will find many ways to use professional tournaments and outings that are held in your area.

Play the host and invite clients or other business associates to an event. The pro tours hold events at various locations across the country. Perhaps one is convenient to you. If not, there may be collegiate golf events, PGA-sponsored junior golf competitions, or skill clinics presented by local pros. Obviously you'll have a better business advantage if you attend with your business associates. But if you can't make it, providing tickets for them will also create goodwill. You have an additional business golf opportunity if your organization sponsors a hospitality tent at any of the pro events.

Work an event. Local outings and pro events depend on volunteers for their success. Working at an event is a great networking tool and a popular way of prospecting for new clients. It will also give you something to talk about with those business associates who love golf.

Non-profit organizations across the country sponsor one-day outings as fund-raisers. Find out what is happening in your area, get involved with the organizations, and volunteer for the golf committee. Get assigned to an activity that will help you reach your business objective. This usually means something with high visibility. Promotion, for example, could be a good choice.

If you work on promoting the event, you may be asked to contact businesses and encourage them to buy foursomes or program ads, sponsor a tee, or donate prizes. This can be just the icebreaker you need to make a business connection you haven't been able to make in any other way. You can follow up and develop the relationship further at the lunch or dinner that typically is part of the outing. Don't worry; you won't have to play. Plenty of volunteers are needed the day of the outing to make sure things run smoothly. And that can provide you with another great business opportunity.

One executive I spoke to is regularly involved with outings sponsored by three different chambers of commerce. She runs a putting contest that every golfer participates in before they start the round. She also donates small prizes such as balls or tees (with her business name and phone number on them) that every participant receives. At the dinner she is a familiar face to everyone present and can easily follow up and begin building business relationships. She prefers this over learning to play because she says she, "Gets to meet everyone, not just one foursome, and the time frame is much more efficient."

Another enterprising non-golfing business golfer I interviewed always volunteers to drive the beverage cart around the course. Because everyone is interested in refreshments, he gets to meet all the participants during the round and can follow up later with those he wants to get to know.

These are just a few examples of the opportunities that exist for even the non-golfer. Learn what is offered in your area. I'm sure you'll find many ways you can use business golf to your advantage. You may enjoy it so much that you'll decide to volunteer for pro events. This is usually a bigger commitment in time and money. The events typically run five to six days and the volunteers are usually required to purchase and wear clothing that identifies them as volunteer staff. The business golf advantages, however, make it well worth it. These events are larger, so you have the opportunity to network with many more people. Representatives of the many corporate sponsors also attend.

In addition to the networking opportunities, you'll also get to see and maybe even meet some of the pros. This makes for great conversation with your business associates who golf. And the impact can be far-reaching geographically, since these events are nationally recognized and often televised. If you are doing business with someone from another part of the country, you can build rapport with a story about how friendly Raymond Floyd was when you met him at a pro event. It is hard to get this kind of mileage out of a story about the local chamber of commerce outing.

As with local outings, choose your volunteer assignment carefully in terms of your business golf objectives. Pro events usually have a large number of volunteer committees. Choose the role that will help you reach your goal.

Also take advantage of the opportunity to attend the event the days you are not scheduled as a volunteer. Invite business associates. You may become an instant celebrity just because you are associated with the event.

If you are not enthusiastic about any of the business golf activities discussed so far, you are probably not destined to be a business golfer. But there are two other options that may work for you, depending on your position within your organization.

Be a sponsor. The commitment here is strictly dollars. Your company name is associated with an event and you gain goodwill through advertising and publicity. You could also sponsor a business associate in a pro-am event. (It would have to be a good client or very valuable employee because pro-am slots are expensive).

Delegate the task. In my interviews I did hear one story about a company that valued business golf so much it hired a scratch golfer from a university golf team to entertain the clients of other employees who did not play. This is the concept behind celebrity golf. But in this case, the scratch golfer was also a qualified business person. I wonder how many clients the non-golfers lost to the scratch golfer. This kind of delegation can be dangerous!

Summary

Some people just don't like golf. If you are one of them, that's fine. There are many alternative sports and social functions that will afford you some of the same opportunities business golf does. But because so many of your clients and business associates probably do enjoy golf, you owe it to yourself to try it. Weigh the business advantages against how you feel about the game before you make your final decision.

Then, with a limited commitment of time and money, you will find that even as a non-golfer, you can still use business golf to great advantage.

Just to Keep Things Interesting . . .
Variations to the Game

As good as vanilla, chocolate, and strawberry are, eventually people wanted something different. So Baskin-Robbins came up with thirty-one flavors. And as interesting and challenging as golf is, it was just a matter of time before inventive golfers created variations of the game. They came up with a lot more than thirty-one!

Even Harry Vardon, who amassed six British Open titles over a twenty year period around the turn of the century and was probably the best known golfer of his time, relied on creative variations to keep the game interesting. In 1913, Vardon and a partner played a round against two javelin throwers! The golfers easily won, even though their competitors only needed to hit within two feet of the cup to hole out.

You won't encounter any javelin throwers as you play business golf, but you will come across many variations to the game. This chapter will cover some of the more common terminology and side games you may need to know. For more information on various games and wagers, read Doug Sanders' book *Action on the First Tee: How to Cash in on Your Favorite Sport* . You'll find a game to suit every occasion and are sure to enjoy Sander's stories about his years on the PGA tour. You'll also get a lot of information about wagering, which is so often a part of golf.

Gambling on the Golf Course

Variations may add interest and challenge to the game, but many golfers believe things don't get really interesting until there's some money riding on it. These golfers believe that wagering makes the round more enjoyable and actually improves their game!

The Hyatt Study found that over two-thirds of the executives surveyed have wagered money on a round of golf. Men are more likely to gamble than women (75 percent compared to 43 percent) and club members gamble more than nonmembers do. The majority of those who gambled (69 percent) said it made the game more enjoyable. Almost half (43 percent) agreed that gambling improved their game.

Sanders says the level of his game improves if some of his own money is at stake. In *Harvey Penick's Little Red Book: Lessons and Teachings from a Lifetime in Golf,* the respected coach shares his belief that even children feel a stronger sense of commitment to learn and are more motivated to practice if a small wager is involved.

Whether or not you consider gambling an important part of golf, you are sure to meet other players who do. So it is important to keep the following tips on gambling etiquette in mind.

- Always understand the game that is proposed. If you are not familiar with it, ask for an explanation. Some of the games can get complicated and the rules may vary in different geographic areas. Also, in some games, there is a lot more money at stake than it may appear. So make sure you know what is going on.
- Be comfortable with the wagering. If you can't afford to lose the maximum that is riding on the round, say so. It is better to tell the others in the foursome that the game is too rich for you and to propose a lower wager than to lose more than you can afford and spoil the day for yourself, and possibly the others.
- Have cash and be prepared to settle up at the end of the round. Depending on the game and the golfers, bets may even be settled at the end of each hole. Whatever you do, don't give out IOUs.
- In business golf, the person with rank and status (the client or the boss) is usually given the honor of suggesting the game and wager.
- The decision on side action typically takes place before the round. Additional games or presses may also be suggested during the round.
- Be a good sport, whether you win or lose. Remember, it is business golf. If the others don't know the etiquette of gambling, be gracious and understanding and stay focused on your objective.
- Understand some of the more common variations. If you are new, you won't be expected to know every game ever invented, but you should be familiar with the favorites.

Basic Side Games

The following variations have been around for years and are widely known. This list is by no means complete. There may be other games that are especially popular in your area, but these are a good starting point.

Match Play or Stroke Play

Match play or stroke play are really formats rather than side games, but can be the basis for wagering. In match play, a winner is decided on each hole and the player or team winning the most holes is the overall winner. Stroke play has one winner, decided by the overall score with every stroke included.

This type of wagering is popular with some business golfers who really aren't into gambling but want some friendly competition. In match play, a low wager can be set for each hole. In both formats, it is not uncommon that lunch may be the prize for the overall winner. At a private club where everything is on the tab, lunch next week might be the prize. This is also a good business golf strategy for setting a follow-up appointment.

Nassau

Nassau is probably the most popular side game around and can be played in either match or stroke play. It actually involves three bets. A $2 Nassau, for example, would mean $2 for the best score (or most holes) on the front nine, $2 for the back nine, and $2 for best overall score. On the surface it would appear that the maximum you could lose in a $2 Nassau is $6. This is true unless there are presses involved. Pressing can increase the stakes very quickly.

Presses

When a player or team is losing for a couple of holes, the game starts to become less interesting. Presses let the losing players get back in the game by setting up second bets.

The foursome may agree before the round that presses are automatic. If they are not, you can't press unless you are two holes down. Pressing can get very complicated and very expensive, so be sure you understand the game your foursome is playing.

In business golf, make certain your business associates understand how this works before you press. Never use a press to psych anyone out or to break their concentration.

Bingo Bango Bongo (Known in Some Areas as Bingle Bangle Bongle)

Bingo Bango Bongo is a popular game because everyone has a chance to win regardless of skill level. On each hole, the person who is first on the green get one point (Bingo); the person who is closest to the cup gets a point (Bango); and the first person to hole out gets a point (Bongo). There are no "gimmes" in this game.

Skins

The Skins Game competition on TV has added to the popularity of this game. The format is the same as on TV, but the stakes are a lot lower. A dollar value is assigned to each hole. The player who wins the hole wins the money. If there is a tie, the money carries over to the next hole.

Low Ball

Low ball is the betting game associated with match play. The golfer with the lowest score on each hole wins.

Longest Drive

As the name suggests, the player with the longest drive on each hole is the winner of the predetermined wager. This game works best when the members of the foursome are closely matched in skill level. Longest drive on a particular hole is a contest used at many outings and often warrants a prize.

Formats and Variations at Outings

Before you attend an outing, you'll want to know the format and variations that will be featured. You'll also want to share this information with any business associates you may invite.

Shotgun Start versus Assigned Tee Times

At outings with a shotgun start, foursomes are assigned to each of the eighteen tees and begin play at the same time, at the sound of a signal. Assigned tee times are just that. Foursomes are slotted to begin the round on the first or tenth tee at a specific time. Depending on when you sign up for an outing, you may or may not have a choice of times.

The obvious advantage to a shotgun start is that everyone finishes at approximately the same time, which can provide greater networking opportunities. Some golfers, however, dislike this format because they prefer playing the course in sequence from the first tee. They also may prefer to play at a certain time of day (many business golfers prefer afternoon tee times). This may not coincide with the shotgun starting time. Be aware of these types of personal preferences when you invite a business associate to an outing.

Playing Formats

Scramble is probably the most popular format because it is fun for players of all skill levels and it is designed to keep the play moving.

Each member of the foursome or team tees off. Then the team captain or members decide which drive was best. All team members then play their second shot from that location and decide which second shot was best. The hole is completed in this manner.

Because everyone is playing as a team, scramble promotes a feeling of camaraderie and is a great networking opportunity. Scramble is also a great format when the business golf objective is team building. It allows the employees to explore the decision-making process and observe the dynamics and interactions that occur when people with different talents and skill levels work together. When used in this way, a debriefing usually takes place to reinforce what was learned during the round.

Best Ball is another favorite format at civic and charity outings. The lowest score recorded by a team member is the score that is posted. Because scores are adjusted for handicaps, players of various skill levels have a chance of posting the lowest sore. Best ball may not hold the interest of new golfers as much as scramble because there is probably less chance of them making a contribution to the team effort.

To keep new players in the game, outings often offer a prize for closest to the pin, which anyone could win. The longest drive contest mentioned earlier is not included at some outings because usually only a few golfers are skilled enough to be in the running.

John Marshall, whose company organizes corporate golf outings, estimates that about 95 percent of all business-related golf events are shotgun starts with a scramble format. However, internal corporate events (no clients, only employees) sometimes have special formats designed specifically to meet certain business golf objectives.

Special Games - Team Building

You may see some of the following variations at outings or as side games in a foursome. But they are often used for formal or informal team building and are often designed to get even the non-golfers involved.

Monkey Golf

Monkey golf originated almost a century ago at Jekyll Island Club in Georgia. The original version was played in teams of ten. Each person selected a club out of the bag, which was the only club they used throughout the round. The team would decide which club was appropriate for each shot and the person who held that club would make the shot.

A modern version involves teams of four, with each player using a single club. One ball is used. The team members play in rotation. Whatever the location or lie of the ball, they must use the club they are carrying. In both versions, the group with the lowest score wins.

The original version is a wonderful team-building, decision-making exercise. The updated version focuses on team dynamics, the group's reaction to individual contributions and the importance of having the proper resources. It is an excellent way to build cohesion in a work team. Both versions are a lot of fun for the participants, in addition to providing a learning experience.

Voodoo Golf

Often featured at resorts, voodoo golf is an excellent way to get both golfers and non-golfers to mix and mingle. Format and rules vary widely, so voodoo golf could be anything from a putting contest to a three-to-nine-hole round - whatever suits the group. The common denominator? Voodoo golf is played at night with glow-in-the-dark clubs and balls! It can be a good team builder because shared laughter is a great way to build bridges between people.

Because internal corporate outings and team-building golf events include many high handicap golfers as well as non-golfers, special rules are often used to make sure everyone will enjoy the event.

Stroke Limits and Maximum Hole Scores

These are common rules at outings with a match or stroke play format. For example, net triple bogey (three above par after adjustment for handicap) could be set as the maximum score. If you reach the maximum, you pick up your ball and use the maximum as your score. This is a great time saver that keeps the game moving and also makes the game less frustrating for new players. To keep the novices interested and in the game, special prizes for accomplishments such as shortest drive and farthest from the hole may be awarded.

Second Chance and Alibi Golf

Second chance and alibi golf allow players do-overs. In second chance, you get one do-over on each hole. Alibi golf permits the number of do-overs equal to your handicap, with the limit of one per hole.

These can be excellent team-building exercises that look at individual behavior in terms of team goals, and the team dynamics that evolve. They can be used to illustrate the impact of team behavior on other teams and on the organization as a whole, since both second chance and alibi golf can slow the pace of the game dramatically.

Blind Holes

In blind holes, the winner is determined on the basis of only nine of the eighteen holes played. The nine holes are selected after everyone has teed off. This is great for keeping everyone involved because there is a chance their "bad" holes won't count.

Blind holes can be an interesting study in team dynamics, especially because the dynamics can change quickly once everyone knows which nine holes will count.

Round-Robins

During a round-robin, each member of the foursome partners with every other player in the group. A common way to do this is to change partners after every six holes. This format allows people to get to know each other better. It also balances things out if there is a big disparity in skill levels. Round-robins work well with a match play format.

String Events

In string events, handicaps are not used, but each person receives a piece of string instead. For new golfers and those who do not have a handicap, one can be assigned as discussed in Chapter 9. The length of string equals one foot for each handicap stroke. You can move the ball at anytime, anywhere a total distance equal to the length of string. However, you cut off a piece of string equal to the distance moved each time you move the ball.

The group dynamics in string events can be very interesting and can lead to insights about how the participants interact at work in terms of decision-making and conflict resolution.

These are just a few of the many variations and formats that can be adapted to the specific needs of a group. Club pros, meeting planners, sales directors at resorts, and companies that specialize in golf outings can help you select the format that best meets the needs of your organization.

Summary

For years golfers have increased their enjoyment of the game through the use of variations and side games, many of which involve wagering. Golf can also be very easily adapted to include employee development and team-building activities that are not only a lot of fun but also provide valuable insights about group dynamics and individual behavior in the work place.

The successful business golfer is aware of the basic formats commonly used throughout the country and knows the etiquette of gambling on the golf course.

The 19th Hole (The Watering Hole)
The Critical Hole in Business Golf

You've putted out on 18, posted your score, visited the locker room, and are ready for the traditional end of the round - the 19th hole. It may involves lunch, dinner, or just a few drinks. Whatever it involves and no matter how you've played the other eighteen, you can still make par (or even get a hole-in-one) on the 19th.

The 19th hole can be the place where you really have a chance to talk business. Or you may not talk business at all. But you'll always have a great opportunity to further solidify the relationship. Just remember what the great golfer Harry Vardon said: Trying to do in three what should normally require four often ends up taking five. It applies to doing business as much as it does to course management. Don't rush the process. Let it develop naturally, based on what has happened to this point.

Think about how a pro hits a shot. It doesn't end when the club hits the ball. There is a follow through that is very critical to the process. It is a natural part of the momentum that starts with the backswing and builds with the forward swing. It brings closure to the entire movement. And there is a sense of flow and connectedness to the entire process.

In business golf, the 19th hole is the follow through to the round. The nature and tone of it will have a connectedness to and flow from the experience of the prior eighteen holes. It will bring a sense of closure to it.

Now think about what a pro does after hitting the shot. Usually, several seconds are spent looking at the shot, even after its flight path has been identified. This helps in planning the strategy for the next shot. But it also allows the pro to savor the shot. Taking the time to stay with the shot for a few seconds before rushing off allows the experience to be imprinted in the mind. This is done in a nonanalytical, intuitive, right-brain way. Positive results are reinforced and less positive results are neutralized. This makes it easier to repeat a successful shot later, because it is imprinted in the mind and body. And taking a few moments this way can also provide a sense of satisfaction and a feeling of centeredness.

In the same way, use the 19th hole to savor the day's events. The shared experience of playing together helps build a relationship. Savoring the events together really strengthens the bond by imprinting the positive experience for both you and your business associate.

Debriefing the Round - Golf Talk

The 19th hole, much like the first eighteen, will be a blend of golf and business. Debriefing the round is usually the first item on the agenda. This is followed by conversation. All this often takes place over drinks, lunch, or dinner, or sometimes over cards. Even if there is no time for the 19th hole, a condensed version of the debriefing will always take place.

Settling Bets

If side games or wagers were part of the round, now is the time to do any final settling up. The cardinal rule is: Winner or loser, be a good sport. If you lost, settle up promptly in cash. IOUs and checks are not considered appropriate.

Occasionally someone in the foursome may suggest continuing the wagering by rolling dice to see who buys the first round of drinks. Other times, someone may casually suggest that the big winner of the wagering is expected to buy. Whether you are the winner or loser, the host or the guest, always be aware of the business politics involved when this kind of situation comes up. Consider the relationship you have with the others. More important, remember the rank and status of the various business associates you are with and the purpose for playing together, and act appropriately.

For example, let's say you are with senior-level executives who are looking you over for a possible promotion. You would assess the situation and act accordingly. If you had a solid relationship with them and were in line for a position that would give you equal status, you might join in the good-natured teasing about the winner buying. But you might decide that you won't be the one to make the suggestion in the first place. On the other hand, if you really don't know the executives very well and they are all several levels above you, you may decide not to actively participate in the teasing. Assess each situation and act accordingly. Situations vary, but the need to be aware of business politics is always present.

The Instant Replays

During the round you may not have time to say much more than, "Nice shot" or "Great putt." And good course management and mental golf skills require that you let go of a bad shot before moving on. So the 19th hole provides the opportunity to relive and comment on any memorable experiences. This sharing is the "savoring the moment" that brings the events of the day into sharper focus and provides a lot of emotional satisfaction.

This is the time for compliments, good-humored bantering, and discussions about the unrelenting nature of the game. Again, keep in mind that this is business. Also be aware of the impact that this sharing can have on a relationship.

When you compliment others, be sincere and specific. Ask questions to call on an associate's expertise if you where really impressed with his or her game. Respond modestly to compliments or questions about how you played. Keep the Monday morning quarterbacking to a minimum. Empathize with others about the poor shots they hit, but keep it light and don't offer advice unless asked.

The debriefing process helps bring closure to the eighteen holes of golf. However, for many serious golfers, complete closure is never reached. They continue to talk about certain shots and holes for years. So the debriefing for this round may include stories about prior rounds. If this is the case, share any stories you may have that are appropriate, but don't dominate the conversation with them.

Use the conversation skills from Chapter 12 during the debriefing. Listen for hot topics, iceberg statements, and other clues. Make a mental note and file them for later use.

As the debriefing process comes to a close, everyone will have a gut level reaction to the experience. The positive response is to want to do it again some time. If someone suggests it, you know you have been successful in creating rapport. If no one suggests it, be sensitive to the business politics and decide if it is appropriate for you to bring it up.

Again assume you are with the senior-level executives who are considering you for that promotion. You probably wouldn't suggest getting together again if you sensed that it would look like you were trying to push your way into the inner circle or fishing for another invitation to play at an exclusive club. If, however, you had played with some of the executives before, you may decide that extending an invitation to play at your club would be appropriate. Then again, could that be perceived as a bribe of sorts to help you get the promotion?

Business politics can get complicated! The best way to handle any situation is to always be aware of the business relationship and the possible impact your behavior can have on your business image. Be sensitive to the verbal and nonverbal cues your associates are sending you. And, if in doubt, the conservative approach is usually best.

Making the Transition to Other Topics

Sometimes the debriefing may be the only 19th hole activity there is time for. With it, you bring closure to the round. Make sure you don't also bring closure to the business relationship! Lay the groundwork for some sort of follow up. This may be as simple as saying you'll talk to the person soon or may actually involve setting up an appointment to discuss business at another time. More on follow up later in the chapter.

In most cases, once the debriefing starts to wind down, someone will introduce a new topic. This may coincide with a change in activity, such as moving from the bar to a table, or deciding to order lunch. You may bring up a new topic when you sense the conversation is lagging or you can wait for someone else to.

Just as the debriefing was the continuation of the round but also gave closure to it, the non-golf conversation during the 19th hole often flows from the conversations started but not completed during the round. Pull out all the mental notes you made on the hot topics, iceberg statements, and key information shared during the first 18 holes. Think of how the various topics fit in with your overall conversation strategy of moving toward talking business. Then modify your strategy for the 19th hole, as necessary.

For example, you may decide that you haven't built enough rapport to discuss business, as you had originally planned. So you would modify your conversation strategy and reintroduce a hot topic that your associate mentioned earlier instead of discussing business. This shows that you were really listening and are genuinely interested. It may also move the relationship to the point at which you *can* talk business. So try to select topics that provide an easy transition to business talk.

Or, your associate may have brought up business during the round, even though you hadn't planned to discuss it. So you'll change your strategy to reintroduce the topic in an appropriate way during the 19th hole. But what exactly is appropriate?

Talking Business

Before you introduce business talk that may lead to doing business, you'll want to access the situation very carefully so you can plan the best strategy possible. When business is lost on the golf course, it is often because this step is overlooked. And business can be lost by missing the cues and being too timid, as well as by misjudging the cues and being too bold.

To see how this works, let's say you are a mortgage banker. An associate from a civic organization you belong to asks you to round out a foursome. You've never met the other two players, but they are friends of your associate. You are playing at a semi-private club and everyone is paying their own green fees and sharing the cost of the carts.

During the round, your associate asks you the direction you think interest rates may be going. The question could be small talk or general business talk. Or, it could be an iceberg question because the person is wondering if this is a good time to refinance his mortgage. You would answer the question without trying to sell or qualify the person as a potential client. But you would pay particular attention to the verbal and nonverbal cues you are getting from the person.

If the person refers back to the topic again later in the round, it could be a clue that he is really thinking seriously of refinancing. This could be a hot prospect! You might say something like, "A lot of people are refinancing and saving a lot of money. If you'd like, I can give you a general idea of the cost-savings breakdown later." This sets the stage for you to follow up.

Now your big decision is how to follow up. Will you talk business during the 19th hole, set up an appointment for a later date or wait and follow up with a phone call later in the week?

Again, you'll want to assess the situation and weigh the appropriateness of discussing business during the 19th hole. Some of the things to consider to help you make your decision are:

- **Does the club allow business talk?** As mentioned in Chapter 7, some private clubs do not. You don't want to embarrass yourself and risk damaging the relationship by discussing business if it is against the club by-laws.
- **What is the goal of this round of business golf?** If you are networking or entertaining a client or prospect, it may be appropriate to discuss business. If you are thanking a client for past business, talking business could be at cross purposes with the goal and may be perceived as manipulative or pushy.
- **How far has your relationship with the person progressed?** Decide if you have established rapport and developed the relationship and the trust bond to the point that your associate is comfortable talking business.
- **What are the business politics?** Carefully consider all the possible overtones of discussing business at this time. For example, if the other person is your host, it may not be appropriate to talk business. Or if someone else in the foursome has started a conversation that is moving toward business, it would not be appro-

priate for you to interrupt. Business politics can be very subtle, so consider all possibilities.

- **Do you have the privacy necessary to discuss business?** If the other two members of the foursome don't join you for the 19th hole, you may decide to talk business. If you are in a club grill and friends are stopping by to chat, you may not have the uninterrupted time needed. And if the 19th hole is the open bar and buffet following an outing, you may find you have absolutely no privacy at all.

- **Do you have enough time and information to discuss business now?** Have you learned enough about the other person's business needs and how your product or service can meet those needs? Can you effectively talk business within the projected time frame? If not, it is best to wait rather than risk damaging the relationship and losing the business.

- **What are your alternatives and the possible outcome of each?** Your options may include: talking business during the 19th hole, mentioning business and setting a follow up appointment, waiting until you are saying your good-byes in the parking lot to set a tentative appointment, or calling later in the week to again debrief the round and possibly bring up business. What is the cost of waiting too long to talk business? For example, if the mortgage banker doesn't reintroduce the topic of refinancing and set an appointment within the next few days, the interest rates could go up and it could actually cost the client money! In most cases, however, the cost of talking business too soon is much greater than the cost of waiting because it could damage the relationship. So weigh your alternatives carefully and make your decision based on the following question.

- **Will discussing business now enhance or detract from the relationship?** Always focus on the other person and the relation ship and how you can be of service to them. This type of client-centered approach will help you with your timing decision.

If you are still in doubt after going through this checklist, it is best to decide on a strategy that will allow you to discuss business at another time. You can use the 19th hole to continue developing rapport by wrapping up the loose ends of any other conversations that were started earlier, and to introduce new topics. However, be sure to lay the groundwork for follow up before the 19th hole is over.

Sinking Your Putt on the 19th

All good things must come to an end, and so too with this round of business golf. Since activities scheduled for the 19th hole vary, so will the length of time spent on the 19th hole. You will, however, have a sense of when things are winding down. All players may putt out and complete the 19th hole together. Or some players may announce they have to leave and not finish it out, just as they had announce they were picking up and not completing one of the other eighteen holes. Whatever the situation, be sure there is a sense of closure brought to the day's activities.

Do this by shaking hands, expressing to everyone that it was an enjoyable day, alluding to doing it again sometime, exchanging business cards with everyone if you haven't already done so, and, if you were a guest, thanking your host. This concludes the round of golf, but there is still another step in a round of business golf.

Developing a Strategy for Your Follow Through

During the 19th hole, you debriefed the round and brought closure to it. You also followed through and did the same for any conversations that were left hanging during the eighteen holes. Now's the time to debrief the entire round of business golf. This is the step that can provide you with valuable information that will contribute to your success in business and in future rounds of business golf. Unfortunately, it is the step that is very often neglected. That is because it takes discipline to shift back into the business mode when you have just wrapped up a relaxing, enjoyable nineteen holes. But taking the few minutes to follow through immediately after the round while memories of the day are still fresh is definitely worth the time you'll spend. Begin by reviewing how you handled the round of golf.

Debrief your round of golf. Did your game enhance or detract from your business golf efforts? Is there a certain aspect of the game you need to focus on and practice more? Are a few lessons in order? What about your course management skills? How did you handle the mental game of golf? Replay the round and decide what, if anything, you need to do to bring your game up to a respectable level.

Next, debrief your round of business golf. Did you reach your objectives for the round? How did your business golf and conversation strategies work out? Did the round contribute to the business image you want to project? If you were the host, were you satisfied with the facility and the arrangements? Is there anything you would do differently the next time? What could you do to improve your effectiveness as a business golfer?

Make notes to update your "Mackay 66". Don't rely on your memory. Jot down anything about your business associate that seems important - personal interests that were mentioned, business and non-business topics that were discussed, specific golf-related information (such as that great chip shot on the 4th hole). This information can be very powerful later in further developing the rapport. You can also use it to customize your message to this particular associate.

Also make some notes about the course or the outing. This can make your future planning a lot easier.

Process the business cards you collected. Have an organized system for storing and retrieving the information you have gathered about the people you've just met. Make notes on the back of the cards to help you remember where and when you met them, how serious they are about golf, any common interests you may have discovered, any business connection there might be, and so forth. Tracking this information will help you expand your recreational golf network as well as your business golf network.

Decide how you'll acknowledge the round. Whether you were the host, the guest, or everyone just got together to play, you'll probably acknowledge the round in some way. It could be as simple as making a comment about what a great day it was. But acknowledging the round is a good way to once again share the moment and in doing so strengthen the bond between you.

If you were the guest, a written thank you is usually in order, although in some cases a phone call may be appropriate. If you were the host, you may follow up with a phone call when you receive a thank you note and reinforce the feeling that a good time was had by all. You might also take the opportunity to advance the relationship further, either with a suggestion to play again sometime or by moving toward business. You'll also decide how and when to follow up with anyone you have just met for the first time. Think about what is appropriate based on your relationship, the reason for playing, and who hosted the round. Then decide on the right acknowledgment and also on if and how to reciprocate.

Decide how you'll reciprocate. Think about how the round of golf affected the relationship and decide if you need to reciprocate and in what way. Sometimes the thank you card may be enough to balance the relationship. In other cases, you may decide you want to invite your host to your club or to an outing. Or you may decide lunch or a small, golf-related gift is more appropriate. The important thing is to think of something that will be appreciated and that will keep the relationship in proper balance.

Tend to your equipment. Prepare your equipment for your next round before you put it away. Clean your clubs and shoes, if this wasn't done after the 18th hole. Make sure you have enough tees, balls, and markers for next time. Take care of any repairs that might be necessary. Replace anything that becomes inconsistent with your business golf image.

Finally, think about your relationship with business golf - and about your next round. You've brought closure to this round of business golf. Now tune in to how you feel about business golf and how and when you want to use it next. Create a momentum for yourself that will let you get the maximum business advantage as well as the maximum enjoyment from the game.

Conclusion

When golf architect Pete Dye designed the TPC at Sawgrass, he brought in small goats to control the weeds the way they do in some areas of Ireland. It didn't occur to Dye that the alligators in Florida would eat the goats! What works well in one situation may not work at all in another. When that happens, modify the plan.

Think about how you can make business golf work most effectively for you. What's right for someone else may not be right for you. Find your own groove in terms of what you enjoy personally and what will work for you professionally. Business golf offers enough flexibility to please just about everyone. Give it a chance to work for you. You may end up in the rough occasionally. But you'll eventually get to the green. And you'll have a lot of fun along the way!

Resource Section

Books on Golf

Playing the Great Game of Golf. Making Every Minute Count. Ken Blanchard. William Morrow & Company, NY. 1992.

Inside Golf. Quotations on the Royal and Ancient Game. Bob Chieger and Pat Sullivan. Macmillan Publishing, NY. 1985.

The Inner Game of Golf. W. Timothy Gallwey. Random House, NY. 1979.

5 Days to Golfing Excellence. Chuck Hogan with Dale Van Dalsem and Susan Davis. Merl Miller & Associates, Lake Oswego, Oregon, 1986.

Golf and the Business Executive: An Attitudinal Study by Hyatt Hotels and Resorts. Chicago. 1993. For further information, contact: Hyatt Corporate Public Relations, 200 West Madison, Chicago, IL 60606.

Corporate Golf Outing Management. John Marshall. Marshall & Associates. Atlanta, GA. 1992. For further information, contact: Marshall & Associates, 3232 Cobb Pkwy, Suite 258, Atlanta, GA 30339.

Golf in the Kingdom. Michael Murphy. Dell, NY. 1973.

Harvey Penick's Little Red Book: Lessons and Teachings from a Lifetime in Golf. Harvey Penick with Bud Shrake. Simon & Schuster, New York. 1992.

Golf Etiquette. Barbara Puett and Jim Apfelbaum. St Martin's Press, New York, 1992.

Action on the First Tee: How to Cash In On Your Favorite Sport. Doug Sanders with Russ Pate. Taylor Publishing, Dallas, TX. 1987.

"And Then Jack Said to Arnie." Don Wade. Contemporary Books, Chicago. 1991.

The PGA Manual of Golf: The Professional's Way to Play Better Golf. Gary Wiren. Macmillan Publishing Company, NY. 1991.

The New Golf Mind. Gary Wiren and Richard Coop with Larry
   Sheehan. Simon & Schuster, NY. 1978.

Additional Golf Resources

- For information on any book ever printed on golf and to be placed
  on the mailing list for a catalog of golf books:

    Richard E. Donovan Enterprises
    P.O. Box 7070
    Endicott, NY 13761

- To learn more about golf networking opportunities for women:

    Executive Women's Golf League
    1401 Forum Way, Suite 100
    West Palm Beach, FL 33401
    (407) 471-1477

- To learn more about your on-course behavioral style, order:

    The Golfer's Profile. $12.00
    Anderson Consulting & Training
    107 Melville Road
    Farmingdale, NY 11735

- The following magazines will help you keep up with the latest in
  golf and will also provide tips to improve your game. There are
  also many regional and local golf periodicals available. Check
  your library.

    Golf Digest
    Golf for Women
    Golf Illustrated
    Golf Magazine
    Golf Journal (publication of the USGA; free with member-
    ship)

- For a quick crash course in the history of golf, visit:

    USGA Museum & Library Golf House
    Liberty Corner Road
    Far Hills, NJ 07931
    (908) 234-2300

PGA World Golf Hall of Fame
PGA Blvd.
Pinehurst, NC 28379
(800) 334-0178

- The United States Golf Association is an excellent source of information on golf topics. The following are a few of the inexpensive booklets business golfers will find helpful. Call 1-800-336-4446 for further information.

> "Golf Rules in Brief"—PG1030. Golf's most basic rules are explained in a six page card format that can be easily carried in your bag.

> "Safety & Etiquette on the Golf Course"—PG1040. Ten page illustrated brochure that provides a crash course on the topic.

> "Baffy Ties Up the Course"—PG1445. An easy-to-read, cartoon format pamphlet that addresses slow play.

> "Handicapping the Unhandicapped"—PG1220. Various methods for handicapping the unhandicapped are described.

> "Tournaments for Your Club"—PG1485. How-to pamphlet listing 36 formats for tournament competition.

> "How to Conduct a Competition"—PG1705. In depth information on all aspects of setting up a competition.

For More Information on . . .
Behavioral Styles, Interpersonal Skills and Business

People Smarts. Bending the Golden Rule to Give Others What They Want. Tony Alessandra and Michael O'Connor with Janice Van Dyke. Pfeiffer and Company, San Diego, CA. 1994.

The 7 Habits of Highly Effective People. Stephen R. Covey. A Fireside Book. Simon & Schuster, New York. 1989.

Gilbert on Greatness. How Sport Psychology Can Make You a Champion. Rob Gilbert. The Center for Sports Success, 91 Belleville Avenue, Bloomfield, New Jersey 07003. 1988.

What to Say When You Talk to Yourself. Shad Helmstetter. Grindle Press, Scottsdale, AZ. 1986.

Swim with the Sharks Without Being Eaten Alive: Outsell, Outman-age, Outmotivate and Outnegotiate Your Competition. Harvey Mackay. William Morrow & Co., New York. 1988.

Beware the Naked Man Who Offers You His Shirt: Do What You Love, Love What You Do, and Deliver More than You Promise. Harvey Mackay. William Morrow & Co., New York. 1990.

What They Don't Teach You at Harvard Business School. Mark McCormack. Bantam Books, New York. 1984.

Unlimited Power. Anthony Robbins. Simon & Schuster, New York. 1986.

Business Etiquette

At Ease Professionally. Hilka Klinkenberg. Bonus Books, Chicago. 1992.

Conversation and Small Talk

How to Start a Conversation and Make Friends. Don Gabor. A Fireside Book. Simon & Schuster, New York. 1983.

Speaking Your Mind in 101 Difficult Situations. Don Gabor. A Fireside Book. Simon & Schuster, New York. 1994.

"50 Ways to Improve Your Conversations" A free tip sheet from Don Gabor. Write: Conversation Arts Media, P.O. Box 150-715, Brooklyn, NY 11215-0008

Networking

The Secrets of Savvy Networking: How to Make the Best Connec-tions—for Business and Personal Success. Susan RoAne. Warner Books, New York. 1993.